Praise fo[r]
The W

"The great value that Jane brings to speakers is to help them drive everything that they do - from marketing to positioning to content - with one unified plan. Jane has my highest recommendation. She sets the standard for excellence as a coach for professional speakers."

Joe Calloway, CSP, CPAE, author of *Becoming a Category of One*

"I've spent tens of thousands of dollars to learn from coaches who taught me half as much as what's written in *The Wealthy Speaker 3.0*. Whether you're just getting started or a seasoned pro, this book is a must-read to master every aspect of your speaking business."

Darryll Stinson, 2 million views 3xTEDx speaker

"Jane's advice was a great resource to grow my speaking business. She helped me make the most of the opportunities I already had, identify new opportunities that I was overlooking and discover the right next steps to SCALE. Any speaker who has Jane in their corner is a speaker who can rely on decades of proven experience and expertise to navigate the speaking business."

Gaby Natale, triple EMMY-winning journalist,
speaker and bestselling author

"In this business if you don't adapt and evolve, you die. And *The Wealthy Speaker 3.0* is just what I needed to help me power up my business and my message. The game has changed. And this book helps you become a game changer too. I have been a fan of Jane's work for years. She has helped many to navigate the speaking industry. So many action steps in this book. Something in here for everybody! I highly recommend it for every speaker from new to seasoned. It's always refreshing when the reputable coaches in this business continue to adapt to the changing needs of the industry. Well done, Jane. This one is a keeper. Now if you will just help me clean out my closets."

Kelly Swanson, author, *Who Hijacked My Fairy Tale?*

"If you're looking for an expert on the professional speaking industry Jane Atkinson is it! Smart, clever and knowledgeable. She is the very best. Listen to her and you will go places!"

Dr. Peter Legge, OBC, author, *Secrets of the Masters*

"Jane Atkinson has done more for speakers' businesses than anyone I know. This book will spread that help to speakers worldwide a thousand times over."

Dave Lieber, *Dallas Morning News* columnist

"Jane has done it again! If you want to shorten your learning curve, fill your calendar and have more impact as a professional speaker, you hold the keys to success in your hands."

Mark LeBlanc, CSP, author of *Never Be the Same* and *Growing Your Business*

JANE ATKINSON

THE Wealthy SPEAKER 3.0

YOUR RECIPE FOR BUILDING THE SPEAKING BUSINESS OF YOUR DREAMS

The material in this publication is provided for information purposes only. Procedures, laws and regulations are constantly changing and the examples given are intended to be general guidelines only. This book is sold with the understanding that no one involved in this publication is attempting herein to render professional advice.

ISBN 978-0-9917512-9-7 (Paperback)
ISBN 978-1-7388089-1-5 (e-Book)

Editor: Catherine Leek of Green Onion Publishing
Cover and Interior Design and Layout: Kim Monteforte of Kim Monteforte Book Design & Self-Publishing Services

Contents

Ingredient I

READY

Ingredient II

AIM

GROWING YOUR BUSINESS – NEXT LEVEL

Foreword

It's a whole new world in the speaking business! It doesn't matter if you are new to the industry or are a speaking veteran, you know the world has shifted drastically. All bets are off and, for the first time in our generation, a global pandemic leveled the playing field for everyone!

What this means is that now is the perfect time to look at your speaking business and decide what you want it to look like. With Jane's help in *The Wealthy Speaker 3.0*, you can adjust your mindset, get clarity on your offerings, and go to market with evidence-based tools. These tools will give you stability even when there are drastic market shifts that could potentially derail your business.

One of the best things about this new book are all the examples of wealthy speakers who used Jane's coaching and principals to up their game and make more money than ever before. Have you noticed that speaking fees have gone up dramatically?

I remember when I first started my business; I would barter with clients who couldn't afford my fee. One of my first events when I went out on my own was for Rubio's Fish Tacos in San Diego. They only had $500 for an after-dinner speech. I was paid $250 in cash, and $250 in fish taco gift certificates! And, I was grateful!

Fast forward to a recent event where a funeral client was short by $5000 of my keynote fee. To make up the difference, they offered me a cremation! My first thought was, "Is there a use-by date?" There is no other industry that I can think of where you can inspire an audience and walk away with afterlife arrangements taken care of!

However, not everyone will barter. There are some speakers who command a high fee and are receiving it on a consistent basis. There is a science behind it, and it starts with your money mindset and goes from there. The good news is that Jane has given you those mindset tools to up your speaker game so you, too, can double and eventually triple your income. Why not? She has proven that people who consistently utilize these tools have amazing results.

You may be thinking, "But, I'm different. I have a unique message. I have a unique business model." Well, I hate to break it to you, but you are not as unique as you think. Jane shows you how you can improve your business if your income is 80% keynotes and 20% book sales and online courses or your business is 50% consulting and 50% coaching and speaking, or any other mix of offerings. It doesn't matter what your business model looks like, Jane has a formula for you to make it work. You are not alone. There is someone out there who was where you are and is now where you want to be. And, because Jane has been in the business for as long as I can remember, she can help you become the wealthy speaker you desire.

Don't just read this book, devour this book. Download the assets, fill out the forms, put them on your wall. Engage Jane as a coach. When I worked with Jane, I improved my mindset about my business and soon I was having what Jane jokingly called "The Year of Marilyn." One year after engaging with Jane as a coach, I was inducted into the National Speaker's CPAE Speaker Hall of Fame. Coincidence? Maybe. But it reminds me of how much mindset is a part of your success as a speaker.

Whether you are a newer speaker coming from the corporate world or a veteran speaker, there is something here for you. The world has changed, and will continue to change and shift. If you're like me, you don't want to be left behind.

There is no better time to be a professional speaker and there is no better coach on the planet to help speakers than Jane Atkinson.

Marilyn Sherman, Hall of Fame business speaker and author of four books including, *Is There a Hole in Your Bucket List*

The Wealthy Speaker Roadmap

Jane's Promise to You

I got into the speaking industry as a business manager/agent for a speaker more than thirty years ago and I feel lucky to be a part of something so important. Some of the world's greatest minds are in our industry and some of the most thought-provoking, inspirational people are out working stages daily and walking the halls of our industry events. They are making the world a better place with their messages.

As you likely know already, our business has its ups and downs, but knowledge is power. The more you know, the more you can compete when the market dips and thrive when the market peaks. I want you to be armed with the best tools a speaker can have - information, ideas, and powerful questions.

I'll be your personal coach, walking you through this proven recipe step by step. And I won't be far away if you need support when you're finished.

The Stitch Strategy Versus the Chocolate Chip Cookie Approach

One of the main reasons we see speakers struggle in today's market is they try to parse or stitch together a strategy on their own. Let me explain.

Business coach Lisa Larter gave me this analogy of the chocolate chip cookie recipe. Imagine you want to bake a batch of chocolate chip cookies. You don't have a family recipe, so you go out on the Internet and search "best chocolate chip cookie recipe." You are going to follow it step by step right?

You wouldn't find ten recipes and take a little from each, would you?

So what about doing the same for your business?

Many speakers will take one idea from YouTube. They might attend a webinar on a subject and adopt an idea or two from that. They'll follow one guru's podcast and use a portion of their method. And then they'll wonder why they didn't get results.

It's because they didn't follow one recipe. One clear path.

So congratulations - you're reading *The Wealthy Speaker 3.0* - you are following one recipe!

Does that mean that this book is your only resource?

No, of course not. But what I would recommend is going all in on this now. After you have soaked up all that you can following this one approach and have your foundation and strategy in place, you can seek expertise in specialty areas (e.g., books, PR, etc.). Hopping around from strategy to strategy will not get you the results that you want.

Hopping around from strategy to strategy will not get you the results that you want.

Can I Customize This Recipe?

Yes, we're going to lay out the Ready, Aim, Launch pieces of the recipe for you - and then you'll customize your approach using the options presented. Please know that there are many, many ways to build a successful speaking business. It's the formula and the order that's important.

There are choices to be made in each section based on what's perfect for you - that's where you'll customize - it's the path that's important. Ready, Aim, Launch is the recipe that we know to have been successful in thousands of speakers' businesses. You'll read more on what each of these means in Chapter 3.

Don't Miss This Opportunity

It is probably well documented (somewhere) that the majority of self-help and business book purchasers buy a book expecting it will change their lives. They read a small number of pages and then put it on their bedside table where it sits with the other six books ... forgotten, gathering dust!

Don't let this book gather dust - you will miss out! You'll miss out on the formula (we call it our "recipe") to help you build the business of your dreams and all of the action items necessary to get there.

Don't let this book gather dust – you will miss out!

I would encourage you, not only to go through this book cover-to-cover one time, but to go back through a second time to build out your "Action Planner" worksheet (see below).

Download These "Can't Miss" Bonuses Now!

Keep your eyes out for this Bonus Download graphic throughout the book that will reference important Worksheets, Coach's Questions, or other bonus materials. In fact, go there right now and download the PDF and, if you have a laser printer, print it off. Many of our readers send the PDF straight to Staples or OfficeMax and have it printed and bound. You will want to refer to it over and over again, so don't wait to grab your download. It's basically a free workbook!

Inside your Bonus Download bundle you will find the Action Planner. This is the most important worksheet in your bonus package. You can read all the books you want, take all the courses and attend every webinar, but if you don't *take action*, then what's the point? Right?

Action is the only thing that matters.

ACTION PLANNER

Action Planner

TO DO
☐ ____________
☐ ____________
☐ ____________
☐ ____________
☐ ____________
☐ ____________
☐ ____________
☐ ____________
☐ ____________
☐ ____________
☐ ____________
☐ ____________
☐ ____________
☐ ____________
☐ ____________
☐ ____________
☐ ____________
☐ ____________
☐ ____________

MY TOP 3 ACTIONS

1. ____________

First Steps:

2. ____________

First Steps:

3. ____________

First Steps:

wealthyspeakerschool.com

COLLECTING THE INGREDIENTS

A Day in the Life of a Wealthy Speaker

Imagine being a professional speaker. Getting paid to speak!

And imagine building the business that's perfect for you.

What's that look like?

Perhaps you are standing on stages in front of hundreds or thousands of people and making an impact. Or maybe you do it from your home studio in your comfy slippers. Imagine that you have a thriving business with an efficient team that operates like a well-oiled machine whether you are on the road speaking or in your home office.

Each engagement that you deliver yields you another two or three spin-off events because you are *just that good*. You often work for clients multiple times, maybe on cross-country tours hitting all of their offices and team members. And those same clients treat you to first-class travel with limo drivers waiting for you at the airport with your name on their sign.

How cool is that?

Envision your books sitting under the seat of every attendee at every event because you pre-sell them with each contract. Picture the amazing relationships you developed in the industry with buyers, speakers' bureaus, and event planners.

When you are building the business of your dreams, what does that look like?

Are you charging a $5,000 fee? $10,000? $30,000? Maybe you're selling packages at five or six figures that include coaching or a course. This is your dream business to build based on what's perfect for you.

And I'm here to tell you that it's possible. And I'm going to show you how.

I have seen it done time and time again, over my thirty-plus years in the speaking business. And I'm going to share dozens of stories of speakers who are living the life of their dreams right now.

I helped them get there and I have no problem tooting their horns. But I'll share my own journey and toot my own horn as well. Why? Because humble has no place here. My intention with this third edition of *The Wealthy Speaker* is to shine brighter than ever before and to attract you toward some of my programs that will help you build the business of your dreams.

Are you ready to get started? Awesome, but first let's get a few things straight ...

1

The Wealthy Speaker Premise

The Wealthy Speaker Reality

The reality of the speaking business is that it's not nearly as glamorous (or easy) as the "Day in the Life of the Wealthy Speaker" scenario outlines. In order to get to first-class air and a limo at every airport you may have to pass through a few Motel 6s and back of the plane (right next to the washroom) flights. There typically (with some exceptions) is no way around the "paying your dues" aspect. And of course, our industry is subject to ups and downs – we typically can't control those.

The bottom line is that this business is not all fully-booked calendars, standing ovations, and juicy paychecks. The thirty minutes that you get to bask in the limelight after a standing O could easily turn into thirty hours of travel nightmare.

But first, what does wealthy even mean?

Defining Wealthy

For the purpose of this book, let me be clear, that "wealthy" is a relative term. There's a small-town fisherman in Mexico who loves his job and his family, and considers himself the wealthiest man on earth. There are speakers who never imagined earning $5,000 for an hour of their time who are over-the-moon feeling wealthy.

What's your definition of wealthy?

Mine is not having to worry about money (I'm there roughly 85% of the time), having a lifestyle that allows for the freedom to work where and when I want, and being healthy enough to enjoy the fruits of my labor with my family. Wealthy to me is also a mindset. It sometimes involves spending $500 to upgrade into the first-class cabin on a plane or train, because I think I'm worth it.

The Road to Wealthy Looks Different for Everyone

My client Ryan Estis started coaching with me back when he still had a day job. He was a Chief Strategy Officer at an Ad Agency and Ryan truly understood business and how leaders could be more successful. As part of his role he started to embrace thought leader marketing and doing industry specific presentations at relevant trade shows and conferences like SHRM (Society for Human Resource Management). He started to get good at it and those eventually became the days he looked forward to the most. And his phone started to ring for speaking inquiries.

Ryan took his craft seriously. He studied and every presentation improved. So did his confidence. He resigned from his corporate career in January 2009 and, given the economy then, the timing could not have been worse. But Ryan had the drive for a speaking career, and he got on the phone and started hustling. Every day he executed consistent actions that all good sales people know are essential. He had a vision. He built relationships. He built a website. He took a risk and hired Lynn, the best salesperson at his previous employer, and they started to grow the business together.

Over a decade later, thousands of speeches, and millions of air miles, Ryan possesses what many speakers dream of, a thriving, two-comma business. Were there bumps along the way? You bet. Ryan had moments of self-doubt, he had health scares, he got burnt out. The road to a million-dollar business has pain in its path, but when you build the lifestyle that is exactly right for you, it can be well worth it.

When I asked Ryan what his biggest lesson was, he said this.

> We need to treat this business like a real business. It requires investment, strategy, resource allocation, budgets, and the right team in order to expand and scale. It also requires that you care deeply for and nurture the product: YOU! The truth is there has never been a better time to be in the expert business. The world is changing so fast and clients need outside perspectives to navigate effectively.

Today when I see Ryan's Instagram feed, with a video of him wakeboarding behind his gorgeous boat, I'm so happy to see him enjoying the fruits of his labor because I know that his definition of wealthy didn't necessarily involve "things." Despite being a seven-figure business owner, for the longest time Ryan didn't even splurge on a new car. He had his own definition of "Wealthy Speaker."

So What's Your Version of the Wealthy Speaker?

Success is subjective. That's why the subtitle of this book is *Your Recipe for Building the Speaking Business of Your Dreams* – emphasis on "your dreams." One speaker's successful year might not appeal to another speaker at all. So it's up to you to decide what success looks like for you. You might only want to speak once a month at a fee of $15,000 or you might want to speak ten times per month at $1,500. We're going to lay out the recipe and you're going to build the business that is perfect for you.

Every speaker has their own set of goals and no one can dictate your goals but you. What I can do, as your coach, is make sure that you are thinking big. After working and living in Texas for six years, I learned how to think bigger.

Will you have to work hard to get to a $15,000 fee? You bet you will, but it's not impossible. Sometimes one major speaking engagement, like the Million Dollar Round Table (MDRT), Meeting Professionals International (MPI), or a major industry conference in your target market, for example the NAPS conference (National Association of Personnel Services), can change the course of a speaker's career.

Or it might be a book that hits the bestseller list, like Kindra Hall's *Stories that Stick* (check the Bonus Download for a link to Kindra's book), which, in part, has brought her to nearly 60,000 followers on Instagram. I've seen things change overnight – but it was years of hard work that led up to the turning point or what we call "Flashpoints" (see later in this Chapter).

Ryan Estis' story is a terrific example of someone who is doing the right things in order to create opportunities. He may have steady growth for several years and then see a major flashpoint when he speaks at a large industry conference or publishes a book. As Henry Hartman says, "Success occurs when preparation meets opportunity."

"Success occurs when preparation meets opportunity."
– Henry Hartman

The First Two Steps to Success in Speaking

I'm going to be outlining the recipe for building the speaking business of your dreams in this book, but there are two foundational pieces that I want to share with you. Two things that I think you cannot miss, two essentials for success, in any business really.

1. Mindset/Belief
2. Consistent Action

Let me explain.

Mindset

For many years, I went about life and business believing that mindset was a portion of someone's success. You know, maybe 50%. But having been trained now in mindset coaching[1] and viewed the successes of my students and coaching clients using those mindset tools, I now believe that mindset at 100% is required. What do I mean by that?

You have to be all in – 100% committed – to the success of your business.

---

[1]I got certified with The Life Coach School using Brooke Castillo's Thought Model in 2021.

FIGURE A:

Two Steps to Success

Step 1

BELIEVE

My Goal: $________________

Step 2

CONSISTENT ACTION

You have to believe in your goal so hard that it hurts. And when you show up at 100%, ready to play, ready to do the work, you will see results. When you invest time, energy, and money into your dream, you are showing your brain that you are committed, and your brain sets out to help you solve problems and clear the path.

If you play small and make decisions from a mindset of "small," you'll have small results.

That's gotta sound hokey to some of you but think of "dabbling in the business" like driving a car with one foot on the brake and one foot on the gas.

A part of this is making your decisions from the place where you have already achieved your goals. If you play small and make decisions from a mindset of "small," you'll have small results.

Let me give you an example. One of my prospective clients (someone who's wanted to work with me for years but won't spend the money) wanted to raise his fee to $10K. Okay, no problem. Let's start investing from a $10K mindset, right? But no, he was going to build his website himself from an inexpensive template and patch together his marketing rather than using a professional web team. Small decisions, small results. Until he turns the corner in his thinking, he will always be holding himself back from bigger paychecks.

So, mindset is essential. Let's move on to the second piece.

Consistent Action

A client came to me one day complaining that they didn't have enough business. "Okay," I said, "let's retrace your steps for the past thirty days. What actions have you taken?"

"Ummmmm. Well, now that I think about it, not that much. I've been busy with this, that, and the other thing."

The students who are kicking butt and taking names at The Wealthy Speaker School right now are people who are taking the right actions *consistently.* What are the right actions?

Right actions could be:

- reaching out to clients,
- building relationships on LinkedIn,
- producing content that your buyers find helpful, or
- working to make the speech better (there's no better form of marketing than a great speech).

Ineffective actions on the other hand might be:

- spending time on social media seeing what other speakers are doing and feeling "less than,"
- developing a program that is outside of your lane to make some quick money, or
- swirling in confusion about what to do next.

When you develop a mindset of 100% belief in your goal (for your dream speaking business) and when you back that up with consistent action, you become unstoppable.

That last piece? We're going to solve here, in this book, for you. You'll have a plethora of ideas to choose from – and all you need to do is take action and move forward. When you develop a mindset of 100% belief in your goal (for your dream speaking business) and when you back that up with consistent action, you become unstoppable.

Coach's Question

How would your life change if you stepped fully into your version of "the Wealthy Speaker?"

The Speaking Industry

Much has changed since I first wrote *The Wealthy Speaker* in 2005. Oh, where to begin!

We've seen economic meltdowns, terrorist attacks, and pandemics, all which have impacted the speaking business greatly. The Pandemic being the most impactful change; it altered the business in a profound way. Companies and speakers have reevaluated everything. Virtual presentations have improved tenfold and have now solidified their place in corporate and association gatherings in the future – not necessarily replacing live events, simply augmenting them. Decision-makers realize now that we can never do without "in person" events because we need human contact, we need community, we need to feel as though we belong to something bigger than ourselves. Fortunately, for our industry, connection will always be needed.

Will a pandemic resurgence or another unknown entity change the industry again? Probably. There are so many unknowns, but all we can do is plug away at building our brand so that if there is another pause in the meetings industry, we are our clients' first call when business comes back. Or, even better, we are able to see opportunities to help our clients while a crisis is occurring. Even in an appalling economy, you can still be a Wealthy Speaker! Sometimes uncertainty means shorter timelines for events and can make cash flow planning more difficult, but hey we'll take it right?

Even in an appalling economy, you can still be a Wealthy Speaker!

My client Meridith Elliott Powell, recently inducted into the Speaking Hall of Fame, sat in the center of the COVD-19 storm and made a decision. I will serve. My clients need me. Here's her story ...

Note: Flashpoint is a term I first heard from Vince Poscente. It refers to a period of significant advancement, like a surge or a flare up of business if you will, in a speaker's career. We're going to share several with you throughout the book. Enjoy Meridith's story.

MERIDITH ELLIOTT POWELL

Finding Opportunity in Crisis

Like so many speakers, 2020 started off strong. By the end of February, I was looking at not only my best quarter ever, but probably my best year since becoming a speaker. Then in one week, the week of March 9, everything changed.

In a matter of days, not only did all of my revenue disappear, but my business model (keynote speaking) became unworkable. Due to the Pandemic, I could no longer get on planes, travel around the world, or engage with thousands of people.

At first, like many of us, I panicked. Unsure of what I was going to do to generate revenue I started to scramble for any idea I could think of – selling things on eBay and even considered delivering pizzas. My panic gave way to anger. Feeling like a victim, I felt like this crisis was happening to me, and it felt so unfair.

Finally, my anger led to action. Not sure what to do or what action to take, I turned to the only thing I could think of. Stop thinking about your own problems, and start focusing on your customers.

The entire transition took about a week. I moved fast, thank goodness, from fear to anger to action.

Understanding my customers would need help, I declared myself an essential worker and started reaching out and just checking-in. Making countless calls every day, I simply listened to how my customers were doing, the challenges they were facing, and paid close attention to what they needed most in order to hold on through the crisis.

I asked simple questions.

- How are things going?
- What are the biggest challenges you're facing?
- How is this crisis impacting you, your customers?
- What changes are happening in your industry?
- What is the biggest obstacle in your way right now?

The key was to focus 100% on the client and what they were going through. I really believed I could be of service, and wanted to find a way to help. I guess you could say I ran into the fire, brought my hose, and was looking for the biggest flames to put out.

The response was unbelievable. Not only were clients willing to talk, they were grateful to have someone listen. Conversation after conversation I was able to find out where my clients' biggest pain points were, how they were managing the challenges, and what they most needed (that they did not have) to solve their problems.

> The conversations lead to the reinvention of my business model. I reached out to help my clients, but honestly they wound up helping me.
>
> By talking and engaging clients, I not only secured current relationships and increased client loyalty, but I found new business – a lot of new business. I created new products and services to solve my clients' problems, and uncovered new opportunity after new opportunity.
>
> Just through having conversations, I would have clients say they were so glad I called. They told me they had been thinking about bringing someone in to speak to their team, or they knew of someone that I should talk with that needed my expertise. I never expected that simply caring about clients could lead to so much opportunity.
>
> Within six months of losing all the business on my 2020 calendar, I had turned my business completely around. My mindset and thoughts drove me into positive action and I saw the results in my bottom line. I experienced my best year on record – crisis and all!

Well done Meridith! Another example of mindset being at the center of a success story.

I spoke to people, just a small handful, who after the Pandemic said they hadn't done one stitch of business in two years. I have to wonder, what if they had changed their mindset from "there's no business for me" to "how can I serve" like Meridith did. How would things have been different?

Why 3.0, Jane?

Over the past thirty years in the speaking industry, what's changed? Well, just about everything. The way we secure business has changed. Technology has advanced. There are new apps and platforms popping up daily. Our CRMs (customer relationship managers) have evolved to now include "pipelines" to predict cash flow and sales. We connect and engage on social media and who would have thought something like TikTok could make someone famous overnight?

What else has changed in the world since I first wrote *The Wealthy Speaker* back in 2005? Think about representation. On stages in the past, especially when I was first starting in the field, you'd see an ocean of middle-aged white guys (no offense guys) and maybe a token female. But now, audiences are demanding inclusion.

Everyone, regardless of race, age, gender, disability, and orientation, should be seen and heard. That's what audiences are expecting now.

That's great news for a lot of people. No matter what our background, we have always had to compete for business, it's just that now the players have changed. I remember Cavett Robert (founder of the National Speakers Association) saying that the pie is big enough for everyone. And it's true. Your goal is to show people the value that you bring to the table so you can find and carve out your niche in the speaking industry – your piece of that pie.

What Else Has Changed?

I've changed. Back when I worked as an agent, helping speakers double their businesses year over year, I had some limiting beliefs about what was possible in the speaking industry – for myself and for others. I knew that you could get to seven figures, but I always thought you had to work really, really hard to get there. As my mindset has evolved so have my ideas around work-life balance and the path to achieving "wealthy."

The way that I teach and coach now reflects my own evolution. If you have ever driven a golf cart, you might know that they put a "governor" on the cart to keep it from going too fast. Well, I feel as though my own "governor" has been removed. I am free to soar as high as I want, while working as much as I want.

The type of mindset coaching that I've been trained in recently has helped me believe in what's possible. If a speaker comes to me currently charging $1500/speech and wants to earn $30,000/speech, I know that it is possible for them to do that with the right formula or recipe. Because remember, it only boils down to two things: mindset (being all in) and consistent action.

Today's Expert

Back in the day, a speaker would be hired because they were a terrific speaker, not necessarily for their expertise. I remember presentations expert Patricia Fripp telling me a story about how clients would book her calendar twelve-to-eighteen months out, but not know what topic they wanted. They just knew that, because she was a terrific speaker, they wanted her. And back then she could do multiple topics. Over time, however, she evolved into an expert in one topic and became known as one of the go-to people in the world of presentation skills. She evolved as the buyers got more sophisticated.

Buyers today often choose their topic first, based on the problems that their organization is having, and then start looking for the person who is the best in that subject-matter, the person who can help solve the problem.

Consider moving away from the "speaker" identity, move to one of being an expert. My friend, speaker, and consultant, Randy Pennington, shared a great analogy with me. Are you the coke, or are you the coke machine? The coke is the product, the expertise. The coke machine is just one way to distribute the product – like a keynote. Speaking is simply one way to distribute our knowledge. We might have books, training, webinars, membership clubs, online courses, etc., that help complement our speaking. All of those are distribution channels, while we remain the expert.

Speaking is simply one way to distribute our knowledge.

What Hasn't Changed?

There is certainly still a need for speakers who provide a particular energy or vibe. A client might need someone to open a conference on a high and set the stage for some learning. Or they may need someone to close who is going to help wrap the learning and theme of the conference into a nice bow and send people home feeling great. Sometimes a speaker is hired simply to make the audience feel something or to remind them of their humanity. And those roles are important.

2

The Wealthy Speaker Mindset

Now, you might be saying, "Come on Jane, just show me how to book gigs." Please bear with me, as this next piece is essential, especially if you have never built wealth or a business before. If you are just adding speaking to an existing seven-figure business, then by all means, you can cruise past this part quickly.

We talked a little about being 100% "in" on your business. A huge part of the Wealthy Speaker equation is being able to accept wealth into your life. You need to condition yourself for success. If you've been successful in other fields, then this isn't going to be much of a challenge for you, but if you've always struggled with building wealth and abundance, then you will continue to struggle unless you change your thinking about money.

Changing Our Thought Patterns

My former boss, Vince Poscente, shared a metaphor many years ago that has stuck with me. Being an Olympic athlete, he studied the power of the mind. He told me that our thoughts are like a river that has been traveling the same route through a valley for many years. The rock and land have been worn away creating the path of least resistance. The water will continue on this path forever unless diverted.

The river represents your thought patterns. Basically, you think the way you've always thought. Perhaps you don't believe that you deserve to be wealthy or you can't possibly buy into the fact that you don't need to work your fingers to the bone in order to earn a nice living.

If you were raised like me, the money conversations often included phrases like "money doesn't grow on trees" along with numerous other sayings that were steeped in "lack." These sayings and attitudes helped build the river of your thoughts in the first place. But then you grow up and attend a seminar by Anthony Robbins or Tim Ferris and you make a decision. "That's it, I'm going to be wealthy. No more messing around." You start the process, but your river continues to take you through the same valley and you find yourself staying in the same state of struggle. So what do you do?

You need to recondition your mind as though you are training for a marathon. To return to Vince's analogy, you are building a dam in order to reroute the water, to create new neuropathways.

Change Your Thoughts, Change Your Results

In 2020, when we were mid-Pandemic, I decided to spend $18,000 to become trained and certified in mindset coaching. Now you might ask "why in the world would you spend this much money when a) it's an awful time to spend money and b) you've already been a coach for twenty years with over 15,000 hours under your belt?" Why??? Well, I'll tell you why.

At the beginning of COVID-19, when all the events were being shut down, I moved into a place of big-time fear. My primary thought was, "My industry has been wiped out." During this time I had been a part of Brooke Castillo's Life Coach School and she tasked us to set an impossible goal. It was to be a short-term goal – two months. Although I thought it was pie in the sky, I took her up on this challenge and set a goal to earn $50,000 over sixty days – what I deemed impossible.

My friend Chris West called me about a week into my task (ten days or so into the Pandemic) and said, "Jane, people need us now more than ever, we should do something." So Chris and I set about doing a four-week Brand Camp. A program that, to this day, is one of the best things

I've ever participated in. Chris carried me in Week 1 of Brand Camp; I was still in fear mode.

BONUS DOWNLOAD

But when I truly embraced and embodied the thought "people need me now more than ever" something magical happened. It was like a light switch had been flipped on in me and my light was shining brighter than ever. Weeks 2, 3, and 4 of Brand Camp, I was back. (Brand Camp is available on my YouTube channel – find the link in the Wealthy Speaker Bonus Download.)

My impossible goal of $50,000 was still looming, but low and behold, I earned that $50K within thirty days of setting the goal. A goal that I thought was utterly impossible came true. It was then that I started to believe that when you change your thoughts, you change your results.

Do I still have to work on my money mindset? Yes, I do. I coach myself around it frequently because the work is never done. I have feelings of self-doubt, but my mindset training is consistent and helps to quell my money worries.

It was then that I started to believe that when you change your thoughts, you change your results.

Back to the $18,000 invested to really learn the thought model and mindset work, I'm happy to say it's been a total game changer for my private coaching clients, Mastermind members, and students in the School. We can teach all the tools but if the mindset piece isn't locked down, we won't see the results. Helping our clients and students shore up their thinking has allowed us to see immediate results that impact their bottom line. Like I said, game changer!

What's Your Money Story?

Remember, mine was "money doesn't grow on trees." My dad was laid off from his job as a structural engineer when he was fifty-five years old and he went into a depression that lasted over a decade. His money worries were constant, when, in fact, he had been so smart with money that my mom still lives quite comfortably to this day, years after his passing. All that worry for nothing.

So "money doesn't grow on trees" meant to me that you had to work hard, really hard, for money. And that became my mindset.

My very first job in the industry, working for a speaker as a business manager, was a money struggle – basement office, three years, straight commission. We did double my speakers' income year over year and my income grew as a result, but it felt like pretty hard work to get there.

Then I was recruited to work for Peter Legge, a magazine magnate out of Vancouver. He had over 100 employees and a $25 million-dollar company. Instead of being in a basement office, I was in the corner office, next to the big boss. Sometimes we flew around in private jets or helicopters. So fun! And we doubled his speaking business year after year. And my income grew exponentially.

But here's the thing. Even though I was often the last to leave the building at night, my old "money struggle" mindset was at play, and I didn't think I deserved to earn a six-figure income. I didn't think I worked hard enough. So what did I do? I blew it up. I sabotaged that job, and quit after two years (Peter and I still miss each other). I started all over again with a speaker who could barely afford me.

My mindset had not caught up with my success. Old patterns allowed me to sabotage myself. Now that setback had a happy ending as I went on to help my third speaker, Vince Poscente of Dallas, TX, move from zero to a million dollars. And I got my income back up enough to purchase my first property. So there are no regrets, just an interesting thing to look back on and notice the self-sabotage that was at play.

Let's examine your money story and see where you might need to re-work the river of your thoughts (see Worksheet 2).

Lifestyle Business

The Wealthy Speaker lifestyle is not necessarily one of private jets and limos. It's actually more of a mentality that leads your business decisions. Creating a lifestyle business is designing a life that allows you to do all of the things that you want to do each day and less of the things that you hate and generating enough income to afford you those choices.

Money Mindset

WHAT IS MY INCOME GOAL?
(by when)

HOW MUCH AM I CURRENTLY MAKING?

WHAT DECISIONS DO I NEED TO STOP MAKING?

WHAT DECISIONS DO I NEED TO START MAKING?

WHAT DO I HAVE GOING FOR ME?
(List all of your assets, smart, talented, expert, etc.)

HOW WILL I SHORE UP MY CONFIDENCE EACH DAY?
(meditate, document wins, use WinStreak app, etc.)

Name: ______________________ Date: ____________

wealthyspeakerschool.com

I interviewed Stephanie Staples on The Wealthy Speaker Podcast last year and it really had an impact on me. She used the term "*lagom*." A Swedish word that means "just the right amount" or "enough." And that was her goal – to have the lifestyle she and her husband wanted, with "enough" income to support it. Her husband retired at 52 and they moved to Vancouver Island (beautiful). They had a financial target that they needed to earn each month in order to live this lifestyle. And they are doing it. Kayaking, speaking, traveling, enjoying life. I love that! It got me thinking about what was "enough" or more than enough for me.

I began my own journey toward "lifestyle business" years ago, after reading Tim Ferris' book, *The 4-Hour Work Week*. I realized I didn't want to be tied so tightly to business, which is why I moved away from managing speakers. You couldn't take off for two weeks when meeting planners and executives wanted to talk to you about booking a deal. You worked to their timelines. As a coach, I can operate my business simply with a laptop and work on my own schedule. (I share this because it might influence your decisions and how much speaking you choose for yourself.)

I can mentor my groups and clients on Zoom when I'm at my cottage for the summer and in Florida (or somewhere south) for several months in the winter. I've designed it so I can now work from anywhere. Travel has always been fun for me, but I have to be honest that post-Pandemic, I have realized that I can be pretty darn happy at home, at the cottage, or in the sunny south during the winter. Having been married over fifteen years now, we have developed into a lovely groove and much of our planning revolves around having fun, our kids, and grandkids. (Six G-kids to date!)

I became aware of my own earning limitations back when coaching was my sole income. Trading your time for money has limits. If my calendar is full, my income is maxed. So first we expanded into products (this book will be book #6) and then into Masterminds and, finally, we opened The Wealthy Speaker School. And after several upgrades, we've got both a course and a group coaching community that is getting our students results. And if desired, we have something that we can scale and sell.

Trading your time for money has limits.

But while all this has been going on, lifestyle has been first and foremost. For years, I have taken Fridays off and had Mondays as a buffer day. Buffer Day is a clean-up messes and solve problems kind of day. In Canada we have one long weekend (holiday Monday) each month in the summer so we often take the week following a long weekend as vacation. (Thank you my friend, Rhonda Scarf, for that idea.)

My team runs the show while I'm gone and I designate ahead of time which day I'm going to check e-mails for an hour or two – usually mid-week. I know it's more difficult to let go of the day to day when you are a speaker who is tied to and doesn't want to miss out on business but it's also important to put your phone away for good stretches of time. Remember, you cannot give from an empty well. So put those autoresponders in place, get a Virtual Assistant to play back up, and schedule some down time.

PERFECT DAY IN YOUR LIFE FIVE YEARS FROM NOW

You may want to keep this worksheet handy; we'll be referring back to it a few times. And once you're finished, you can post it somewhere prominent and look at it regularly. Olympic athletes swear by visualization exercises and, since they make it to the Olympics, I guess they must work!

Go back to A Day in the Life of a Wealthy Speaker (page 7) and read it again. Use it to be inspired, to generate ideas of what you'd love in your business. Now write down what your perfect day looks like five years from now (if five years feels too long, use three years, or one year).

Write down all of the details. Who do you speak for? Or consult with? At what fee? What are the results? How does that feel? What type of audience is it? What do your home and office life look like? Do you have a vacation house? Where is it? How much time do you spend there? Where else do you go for vacation? Do you have products? What are your passive income streams? What do your personal relationships look like? What kind of fun are you and your family having? Are you healthy? Who's in your corner and on your team?

Don't leave out any detail – this is your perfect day.

Perfect Day in Your Life Five Years from Now

INSTRUCTIONS: Imagine you're having the perfect day in your life, 5 years from now. What does that look like? *(e.g., Who is around you? Where do you travel? How often do you speak? At what fee? What are your other sources of revenue? What do you do in your free time?, etc.)*

wealthyspeakerschool.com

Perfect Day in Your Life Five Years from Now

(Continued...)

wealthyspeakerschool.com

Once you have completed the exercise, place it in a prominent place and review it daily. Make it a part of your morning ritual. Allow the principle of "you become what you think about most of the time" to work in your favor.

Imagine the possibilities!!!

JEN MCDONOUGH

From Soul-Sucking Job to Vacation Property

Sitting in my fifteen-year-old blue minivan on the third-floor parking ramp during my lunch break, I clung to my cell phone. These calls were (literally) my lifeline of hope to a better future. I had joined The Wealthy Speaker School and call after call I would listen intently as Jane shared lessons on how to become a wealthy speaker.

My breath was thick as fog from the sub-zero Minnesota temperatures that left my fingers and toes numb (I wouldn't turn the heat on, fearing I would miss something important due to the noise). Sitting there shivering, there were times it was very hard to really believe I could get paid to speak.

Before joining Jane's school, my secret fear was that I would be stuck in my soul-sucking job with the golden handcuffs forever, when my goal was to be out on my own. The fear of failure from trying was present, however, the fear of being stuck in my job for another decade was more terrifying for me.

I first started in the school while my family and I were in the midst of paying off a mountain load of debt and medical expenses (over $212K worth of debt paid in four years). We were raising four kids (one with a medical condition) and taking on side jobs in addition to our full-time jobs that came with a two-hour daily commute. So you can only imagine how any money (and time) invested in anything was a huge deal as every dollar was being looked at carefully.

I struggled with doubt, uncertainty, w discomfort. Would I actually be able to do this? Who was I to think this was possible? Why would someone hire me? These were questions that lodged in the back of my mind especially as having a speaking business was definitely not the nine-to-five, don't color outside the lines story I was raised to believe.

Having become an eight-time national weightlifter, two-time U.S. Olympic Festival medal winner and MN Hall of Fame athlete after starting to lift with just a broomstick, I understood the value of having the *best* coaches surround me while I built my speaking business from the ground up. Thus the decision to join Jane's school – I was a newbie and desired to learn the business from the best. Looking back, it was one of the wisest things I could have done for my speaking business as it saved me so much time, money, and effort in the long run.

As I sit here writing this I am looking out from the windows of our newest purchase. A beautiful four-bedroom log home that sits on ten acres of woods that is home to Minnesota's best fishing, lakes, and parks. I can't help but be in immense gratitude to Jane and the school for guiding me along the journey of building this business. Getting to learn the Wealthy Speaker Recipe was really a true gift as the teachings have taken our family to new heights, not only in terms of money, but also in terms of lifestyle. To actually be paid for doing what I love and getting to impact the world around us in a positive way... well, let me just tell you my friends, it just doesn't get much better than this. And when the driver is waiting at the airport with a sign with your name on it, well, that's just icing.

The journey and keys to building a six-figure speaking business certainly didn't happen magically overnight. It took consistent action, combined with having a strong mindset and surrounding myself with the best in the business.

The joy of finding that sweet spot where passion meets profit is truly a beautiful thing.

While the road was filled with failure and discomfort, I will tell you in all honesty the joy of finding that sweet spot where passion meets profit is truly a beautiful thing and makes everything all worth it in the end.

So when times get tough, remember that just past fear, doubt, and uncertainty is where excitement and adventure reside.

I had watched Jen grow and evolve inside the school and thought, "Damn, she's a superstar! She's getting booked all over the place." And you know, part of being an entrepreneur is identifying talent. Long before I was ready, I hired Jen to become a part of our faculty. Today, over a decade later, Jen balances the life of a busy speaker with helping our students succeed. (Someday, I hope she'll come in off the road and run our School.) Having someone who understands how to get booked doing the teaching is so beneficial to our students. And the delightful side benefit has been watching Jen and her family living their dream version of the Wealthy Speaker lifestyle.

As a side tip: Always be keeping your eye out for talent, you never know what kind of loyalty will come from helping someone leave their soul-sucking job ahead of schedule.

Coach's Question

Who do I need to become to be a Wealthy Speaker?

Your Morning Routine – An Essential Factor

When it comes to keeping a mind-body balance, an essential factor for a wealthy speaker, how you start your day will dictate how your day goes.

An intentional start to the day means you have a better chance of not seeing your day go off the rails. Some of the keys to getting your day started well might include journaling, reading something positive and helpful, exercise, meditation, prayer, etc. Many of the wealthiest people in the world start their day with some of these activities. They start their day with intention.

I believe in this so much that I developed *The Wealthy Speaker Daily Success Planner and Journal.* It's the perfect way to ensure that your day starts confidently, and on the right foot. We'll put a link to it in the Bonus PDF.

Your Thought Model – An Important Tool for Speakers

The Thought Model

I want to share this thought model with you that I learned from Brooke Castillo. You might scoff at the idea of "thought work" but I've watched Brooke's business scale from $1 million to $10 million and, at the time of this printing, to $50 million. I've learned from her mistakes (and there have been a few along the way) and I've learned from her teaching. If you'd like to follow her work, check out Brooke's podcast called "The Life Coach School Podcast." (It's best to start with the earliest episodes to learn the basics of The Thought Model.) Her teachings and style aren't for everyone, but I have come to appreciate what she brings to the table.

Perhaps you've heard of The Thought Model, or have already used something like it. I like the way Brooke uses it. So much so that I got certified in this work during the Pandemic. Remember that story about me spending $18K during COVID?

Why? Because it makes my clients unstoppable. If they can manage their thoughts, the sky's the limit.

Here's the breakdown:

C = Circumstances

T = Thoughts

F = Feelings

A = Actions

R = Results

- **Circumstances.** Are the things that happen in the world around us – things that we don't control. They are factual. Examples include the weather, our past, other people's behavior, the economy, pandemics. We treat circumstances as neutral because (most times) we cannot change them. This falls right in line with that old saying, "It's not what happens to you (circumstances), it's what you do about it." It should really be, "It's what you *think* about it."

- **Thoughts.** Are the sentences that constantly run through our minds. Sometimes we are aware of our thoughts, but often we aren't. Examples include, "I'm not getting paid enough," or "I'll never get there," or "The client will not be able to afford my fee." You see how powerful it might be to change our thoughts? We can't always change circumstances, but we can change our thoughts about the circumstances.

We can't always change circumstances, but we can change our thoughts about the circumstances.

- **Feelings.** Are the emotions we feel in our bodies and they're directly related to the thoughts we are thinking. Examples include dejection, sadness, pride, excitement. Emotions are voluntary because we can change what we feel by changing our thoughts.

- **Actions.** Refer to behaviors, reactions, or inaction. They are directly related to our feelings. An example might be you think the clients don't have any money to pay you, so you don't pick up the phone to ask. Or perhaps you come from a positive thought and take all of the actions we lay out in this book.

- **Results.** Are the effects of our actions. Perhaps you have taken all the right actions, and over time, like Jen's example earlier, you get results.

Let's run this thought, "I don't know who is going to book me" through our Thought Model (see Figure B). Our goal is to move from an unintentional model (thought) to an intentional one. You'll find a blank version of Figure B in the Wealthy Speaker Bonus Download.

When we get in the habit of noticing our thoughts, and understanding that our thoughts equal our results, we are able to make the adjustments and create feelings that will drive actions. When you take actions from a place of "less than" in terms of confidence, your results will be compromised.

FIGURE B:

The Thought Model Example

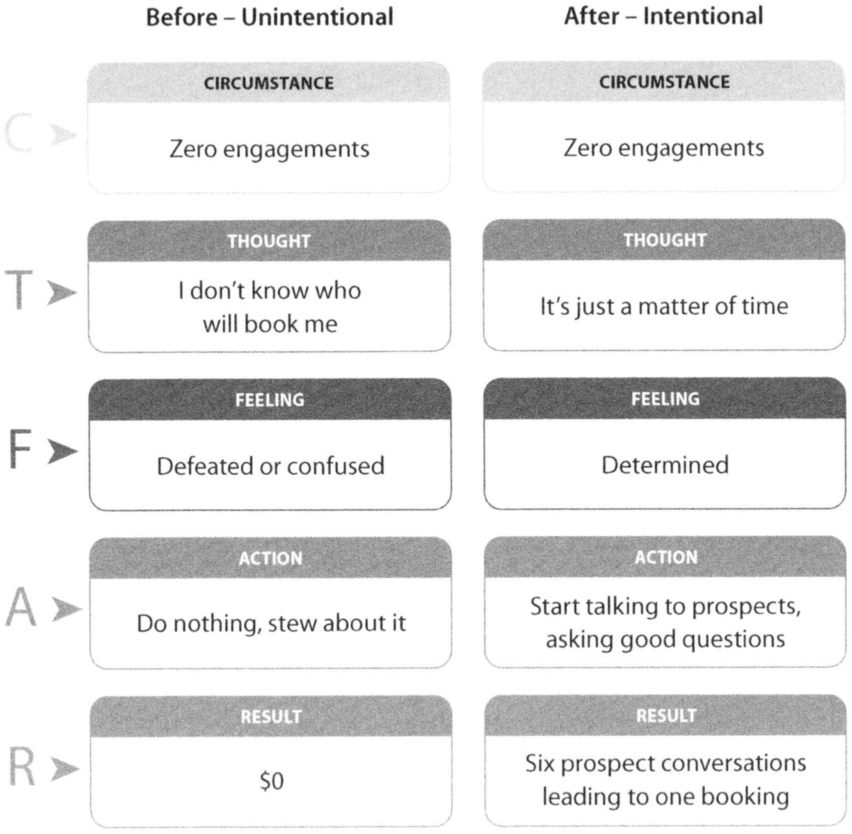

- Circumstances may happen (i.e., pandemic), but your thoughts about them are optional. Remember Meridith's story?
- You can start from the results you want and work backwards. For instance, "What thought do I need to have in order to earn $50,000 in revenue this _____ month/this year?"
- Check in on your thoughts prior to hopping on a client negotiation. Are you prepared to stand tall in your value and your fees? Or are you coming from a place of lack or uncertainty.
- When you've had a difficult month financially, circle back and ask, "What was my Thought this month?" It might surprise you.

- If needed, dust off some of your old books about thinking, such as *The Power of Positive Thinking* by Norman Vincent Peale, *Think and Grow Rich* by Napoleon Hill and the more recent *Mindset* by Carol Dweck.

Hopping Off the Struggle Bus

The students in our School often fall into one of two categories - one of struggle or one of determination. Now, of course, everyone goes through challenging times, but I've come to realize that it's difficult to change someone's mindset without putting in the work. We've all heard of "glass half empty" people. If you know you are a GHE, then really start to acknowledge your thoughts and put them down on paper so that they have less power over you. Switching from an "unintentional" thought to an "intentional" thought may feel like a Band-Aid approach when there are decades of negative mindset to undo, but becoming aware that "maybe this is just a thought I'm having" and making room for the notion that perhaps it's untrue can be a healthy first step.

When you take actions from a place of "less than" in terms of confidence, your results will be compromised.

3

The Wealthy Speaker Recipe

Ingredients of the Wealthy Speaker Process

Okay, we're here! Now that we have our mindset and lifestyle mapped out, let's get down to the fun stuff!

Figure C outlines the steps that we'll take walking through the Ready, Aim, Launch process. No matter how far along you are in your career, it's never too late to go back to the beginning and ensure that you are on the right track – especially if you are not getting all of the business you want.

In the case of an experienced speaker, you're already cooking, possibly at full heat. With a few minor adjustments, we'll just help you substitute ingredients that get better results, preferably without reducing the temperature. In the case of the beginning speaker, we'll go step by step through the ingredients so that you are confident about what you bring to the market before you start launching marketing programs. Let's bake those cookies baby!

Coach's Question

What is going to get in my way of starting this business?

What can I do now, or plan to do, to ensure that I continue to move forward?

FIGURE C:

The Wealthy Speaker Recipe

Here's a quick breakdown and an overview of the focus of each of the ingredients – Ready, Aim, Launch – in the Wealthy Speaker Recipe.

READY

This the *clarity* phase. We'll get crystal clear on what you are selling, who your ideal audience is and how much you are going to charge. (See I told you this was the fun part!)

AIM

This is the *marketing* phase. And because the best form of marketing is an epic presentation, combined with an effective website, we include terrific sections on presentation skills and building your site. We'll also break down some myths of speaker marketing, your social media strategy, and what you'll need on your demo video.

LAUNCH

This is where we *roll out* to your target audience. You'll Launch your outbound efforts and develop a sales and marketing funnel that will put you in the position to get booked. This is where the fun expands because it's the "show me the money" stage!

READY	AIM	LAUNCH
Get crystal clear on what you're selling, pick a lane, develop a promise.	Build website and video. Develop the speech.	Roll out to target markets, build sales funnel.
CLARITY	**MARKETING**	**ROLL OUT**

What's Getting in Your Way?

Several years back, my coaching client, Ron, was a successful corporate man. He had climbed to VP of several Fortune 500 companies and was launching his speaking business. Every month Ron and I would have our coaching call and Ron would give me a list of reasons explaining why he hadn't accomplished anything. I allowed this to go on for a couple of months and then I posed the big question, "What's stopping you from moving forward in your speaking career?" When Ron took an honest look at the situation, he realized that he was sabotaging himself. Why?

He was afraid of stepping into something so foreign. After all, he was used to being the leader, the guy with the solid reputation, the golden boy that his company could count on. Now, no one would know him, he had to start over to build a reputation and that, understandably, was scary.

Ron couldn't (or wouldn't) take any of the actions necessary to get started until he addressed his uncertain mindset. Ron was letting the negative thought, "I don't know how to do this," derail his dream of building a speaking business.

Once we established a new thought for Ron, "I *know* how to do hard things, I've done them before," and he started taking action on all of the things we mapped out for him – using Ready, Aim, Launch – he was off to the races. Today Ron has a thriving speaking business.

Coach's Question

How will you move through fear of the unknown if/when it hits?

Ready, Aim, & Launch with Strategy

Have you ever put together a marketing campaign or new product or program that was a total flop? I have. Have you ever blown several hundred, or several thousand, dollars on an idea that just didn't work? I have. In fact I cannot tell you how many times I should have run through the questions in Figure D (below). And didn't.

Just because you can do it, doesn't mean you should.

There's a saying that someone smart (sorry can't recall who) once shared with me. Just because you can do it, doesn't mean you should.

One of my coaching clients, Carmen, was getting ready to launch her business into the college market. She had been helping young adults learn how to be more resilient. During a coaching session she asked what I thought about running a mentoring program to help people write books. It was top of mind for her because she had just finished her second book. She could do it – easily – but was it in line with her long-term vision for her business? Would attracting budding authors be beneficial to her cause? We decided together – probably not.

Years ago, I had an idea in my head for a book. This would have been my second or third book. Had I had a coach, or the tool below, I may not have written it. I wrote a book called *The Frog Whisperer.* It was all about how to find true love. It was born from my private struggle kissing frog after frog and when I put a strategy into place, I finally met and married my prince. (I use that term loosely, because I'm clear that most women do not want or need a prince to come to our "rescue.")

This book felt like it needed to get out of my head and onto paper, but, when it came to promoting the book, I realized that I didn't want to be coaching people on their love lives, I didn't want to be known as a "love" expert. And I didn't really want to promote the book. It was totally outside my lane and made no sense. I've since put this book on Kindle only and if I had my time (and money) back I would not have written that book. And I definitely wouldn't have created journals and CDs as companion pieces – all of which went into a giant recycling bin (ouch) about ten years after writing a book that was not in line with my strategy.

Keep this tool handy and use the Idea Filter to identify when you are heading down rabbit holes that will lead you away from your goals rather than towards. I based this loosely on a tool that Dan Sullivan's Strategic Coach uses, called the Impact Filter, and adjusted it for our industry.

FIGURE D:

Idea Filter

Run your ideas through the filter before you put them into action.

1. Can I afford this idea? ☐ Yes ☐ No
2. Does it fit with my overall business strategy (or is it outside my lane)? ☐ Yes ☐ No
3. Do I have what it takes to implement this idea successfully? ☐ Yes ☐ No
4. Will it take me away from higher priority work? ☐ Yes ☐ No
5. Who needs to be involved?

____

____

6. How will I measure success on this goal?

____

____

____

7. Will this idea get me closer to my ultimate goal (or is it a distraction)?

____

____

8. What is the payoff?

____

____

____

9. What is my intention?

____

____

____

BONUS DOWNLOAD

Those few basic questions will help you evaluate your existing ideas as well as the ones in this book. From here on, I'm going to walk you through much of the process so you won't be shooting randomly any more.

Taking Action

About a year ago in our Mastermind, one of our members, Jo, was complaining to her coach that she was unhappy with her progress. When the coach investigated further it turned out that Jo had a long list of action items. But they didn't get acted upon. Because of a busy day job and some personal matters at home, Jo hadn't been able to move the needle.

Now, there are going to be times in your life, like Jo's, when you are going to lose focus. Personal items like caring for a sick child or parent take priority. So Jo just needed to give herself some grace, move the ball forward in small increments and stop beating herself up. The key to this is recognizing when things have been accomplished.

Note: Today, Jo is launched and booking business, and had she given up during her times of impatience, she would not be living the dream. One of the tools Jo used was Dan Sullivan's Win Streak App spawned from his book, *The Gap and The Gain.* Make sure to check those out.

It's not enough to take a course, read a book, or listen to a webinar, you've got to put it into action.

BONUS DOWNLOAD

It's not enough to take a course, read a book, or listen to a webinar, you've got to put it into action. Bottom line for you, dear reader, is you can't only read this book, you've got to put it into action.

Action Steps

I suggest three key techniques for taking action.

1. Keep your to do list handy (Worksheet 4, Action Planner).
2. Move each item to your daily calendar to get stuff done.
3. Recognize yourself for your accomplishments. It's the best way to build momentum.

ACTION PLANNER

Action Planner

TO DO
☐ ______
☐ ______
☐ ______
☐ ______
☐ ______
☐ ______
☐ ______
☐ ______
☐ ______
☐ ______
☐ ______
☐ ______
☐ ______
☐ ______
☐ ______
☐ ______
☐ ______
☐ ______
☐ ______

MY TOP 3 ACTIONS

1. ______

First Steps:

2. ______

First Steps:

3. ______

First Steps:

wealthyspeakerschool.com

In each phase of the Wealthy Speaker Recipe, there will be action steps – tasks that must be completed in order for you to move forward and start building momentum. For example, in Ingredient I: Ready, where you are focusing on what you are selling (see Chapter 5), an action item might be to take your speech idea to a few of your colleagues or prospective clients to see if they would buy it. Or you may join Toastmasters so that you have a place to practice new speech material.

Don't allow the "to dos" that pop into your head as you are reading distract you from the process. Keep your Action Planner worksheet at your side, and put things on your list, so that you can continue to move forward.

From Plan to Action

An important step in the process is to move your "First Steps" tasks onto your day-to-day calendar and make sure you complete them. You'll be surprised at how quickly you can move your business forward, one calendar entry at a time. Try to be patient. Building a business – any business – takes time and consistent action.

In fact, placing two or three hours of "work on speaking business" on your calendar as many days a week as you can afford will help you build and keep momentum. If you have a distraction because life pops up, get right back to it as soon as you can.

The Value of Coaching

Having a coach at your side can be a total game changer; it has been for me. I often have a one-on-one business coach I meet with quarterly. I have been a part of Dan Sullivan's Strategic Coach (group coaching) for over a decade. Because of my coaches, I have already increased my business tenfold once, and have created goals far loftier than I would have ever imagined. My coaches saw big things for me far sooner than I would have identified on my own.

BONUS DOWNLOAD

Our students in The Wealthy Speaker School are all going through the Ready, Aim, Launch courses and, while they are doing that, they get group coaching several times per month.

Doing this work can be daunting without any support. Between the community message board and the coaches, our students have all the support they need to move through the process to results.

If you are an emerging speaker, definitely take a look at The Wealthy Speaker School. And if you are more advanced or want to move at a faster pace, schedule a chat with us about our Masterminds or private coaching. Our programs are invaluable and can shave years off your learning and growth curves.

I'm a big believer that if you want to be the best, hire the best, so that's what I do. I hope you will too.

Find Study Buddies

One of the most powerful things I see happening inside The Wealthy Speaker School is the formation of smaller groups of two or more people who help to encourage each other on their journey. Accountability partners pair off and move towards their dream. It's a beautiful thing. We also see people asking questions and sharing best practices, leads, and paid business.

My suggestion is that if you don't have a support system for speaking in place, start your own group or find one or two people who are on the same journey. This can be a lonely business.

Coach's Question

Who do I want to have with me, on my team, for this journey?

4

Getting Ready for Market

My Motivation

Coach's Question

Why do I want to be a speaker? What is really motivating this career choice?

Kendal Netmaker, my client, is an indigenous entrepreneur who grew up with a single mom living on a First Nations' reservation. Someone in his life (the dad of a friend) saw his potential and invested in him. This was the beginning of his journey to create an abundant life. When I met Kendal, he was a retail business owner, struggling to balance it all, but he knew he had a message to share. Fast forward several years, I have to tell you that watching him evolve has been a gift to me. Here's his advice for you.

KENDAL NETMAKER

Kendal Netmaker – The Slow Burn to Success

Having had a successful retail business, I was getting asked to speak. When I first started working with Jane four years ago, I was lacking clarity and was lucky to pull off a $5000 keynote. This business takes time. And year after year I would get better. Better on the platform, better in my business. I have focused non-stop on creating a world-class speaking business that allows me the freedom to be with my wife and two children. And to share my message with thousands.

That slow burn, moving the needle year after year, has paid off. I have been awarded Canada's Top 40 Under 40, a Communications & Leadership Award from Toastmasters Canada, and we have surpassed seven figures in keynote speaking revenue.

It takes three to five years to launch a successful speaking business.

One of my tactics for getting to new heights in my business has been to hire the best coaches and follow their strategy. The bottom line is that it takes time and energy. It takes three to five years to launch a successful speaking business. The result is that I get to help change the world, one audience at a time.

Types of Speakers

Motivational Versus Inspirational

There are a lot of decisions to make along the way when setting up a speaking business. And some of you might be thinking, "I want to be a motivational speaker." I have good news for you. Although motivational speakers got a bad rap for a few years (people thought they were all fluff and no return on investment), motivation has come back around. Why? Because it has its place in meetings and conferences. A great motivational opening keynote can set the stage for an entire conference. While a terrific closing will send everyone home from the event pumped and ready to take action. Those roles are important.

While we still want to be seen as an expert, the motivation can run along simultaneously. An example of this approach is Darryl Stinson, an associate coach in our school. Darryl, a former Division I athlete, survived a suicide attempt to go on to change people's lives as a motivational style speaker. His theme is "Turn Your Message into a Movement" so he has an expertise, but he runs a motivational message underneath.

So you are not really choosing one over the other. In my mind, the difference between motivational and inspirational is that the former is more designed for action taking – this is my recipe for success – and the latter says my story will inspire you and provoke thought. Both are necessary.

All speaking can, and should, include your expertise, underlined by your story and/or some motivational calls to action.

Speaking Versus Training

Even though this book was written mainly with keynote speaking in mind, we really cover the entire gamut of a speaking business. Many keynote speakers have training programs, workshops, consulting, and seminars in their product line. At the same time, there are speakers who deliver only keynote speeches. Much of my experience is with keynoting, although many of the speakers in our school are focused primarily on training and workshops. This recipe, Ready, Aim, Launch, works for all different types of business models.

In the early stages of your career, you might explore the training arena in order to precisely identify your specialty or niche. I've coached dozens of speakers who went to work for training companies in order to pay their dues. Also, I have known many speakers who want to transition out of training into full-time keynoting, simply because the training avenue is much more demanding (full days versus sixty minutes). For those considering a Fred Pryor type of path, please note that most training companies pay a fraction of what you can charge on your own (e.g., $500/day vs. $5,000/day).

Most training companies pay a fraction of what you can charge on your own (e.g., $500/day vs. $5,000/day).

Business Model Options

There are few speakers who do business in exactly the same way and that is what's great about this industry. Perhaps you will come from another industry and invent an entirely new business model. *Bravo* – be different, be brave.

Some sample business models being used today are outlined below. These are suggestions and, like everything in this book, use what works for you.

- 80% keynotes, 20% product sales (books, online course)
- 25% keynotes, 50% consulting, 25% product sales
- 75% training, 15% webinars (paid), 10% podcast (sponsors)
- 50% training, 25% coaching, 25% keynotes
- 50% consulting, 20% speaking, 30% membership and product sales
- 70% coaching, 10% product sales, 20% public seminars
- 90% community and product sales, 10% keynotes

MARIE-HELENE PELLETIER

A Business Model that Works for You

Marie-Helene Pelletier (who goes by MH), PhD, MBA, psychologist, has a thriving speaking business focused on resilience in the workplace. Because of her science and research credentials, doctors and health-care audiences took to her immediately. And financial industry leaders value their access to a working psychologist with a business mind – they know she gets them.

She's also bilingual (French and English), which makes her even more of a unicorn. As demand increased, she started to expand her offerings. Her repertoire now includes customized training – with some clients hiring her several years in a row – virtual workshops, and a new book.

Dr. MH also keeps a professional coaching practice, and aims for a specific mix of in-person and virtual speaking engagements to carry out both individual and group work. She adjusts as demand grows. The business is turning out to be exactly what MH envisioned. As she expands her speaking work and grows her team, she'll be adding more to her menu of offerings in the months and years ahead.

Your Business Model

Think of your business model as your empire. And you can build it as big or as small as you like (see Worksheet 5 coming up in this section). My advice, for those who want to become truly wealthy in money terms, however, is that you build a bustling empire with several revenue streams – not just speaking. Trading time for money has its limits.

If you have a lot on your plate already, you may need to "clear some land" for your empire.

If you have a lot on your plate already, you may need to "clear some land" for your empire. Trying to launch a second income stream while barely managing the first is difficult. Consider what you need to drop to make room or clear the land. Do you have commitments that need to go away? A volunteer position that's gotten out of hand? Is there a child care snafu that needs to be solved before you begin to build your empire?

Should I Keep My Day Job?

Speaking of clearing the land for your empire, you might be wondering, should I keep my job? If you have a day job that isn't crushing your spirit every day like Jen's, we recommend that you keep it for another year or so. Why? Because when you approach your prospects from anything that smacks of desperation (I "need" to make money vs. I'd love to share my wisdom with you), you'll be sending out the wrong signals. Having financial security while building your business is the best-case scenario. And the most opportune time to leave your job is when you have enough revenue from speaking to replace your paycheck. If you crave stability, you will have to mentally prepare for the seasonal ups and downs of a speaking business.

The most opportune time to leave your job is when you have enough revenue from speaking to replace your paycheck.

If you have already quit your job, look at that as a positive as well because now you'll have the time and energy to build a new business. But check out question #4 in the Start-Up Speaker's Quiz (see Worksheet 6, a little further along in this Chapter) to be sure you can handle the financial realities of the start-up.

Your business model will help you stay focused. Your lane or expertise could be one word like "communication." This is just for you to see, so just use a word that helps glue all of your ideas together.

BUSINESS MODEL BUILDER

BONUS DOWNLOAD

THE WEALTHY SPEAKER SCHOOL
Build The Speaking Business of Your Dreams

Business Model Builder

Name: ______________ Date: ______________

MY LANE/EXPERTISE

____

RAINMAKER #1

RAINMAKER #2

PRODUCT/ SERVICE

INCOME:

PRODUCT/ SERVICE

INCOME:

PRODUCT/ SERVICE

INCOME:

PRODUCT/ SERVICE

INCOME:

PRODUCT/ SERVICE

INCOME:

TOTAL INCOME:

wealthyspeakerschool.com

The rainmakers are the products or services that you'll offer that will lead to more business in other places. It might be that your book leads to keynotes. Or your keynotes lead to book sales. But if you are only offering one thing, say keynotes, that's okay. It will go in two places.

Under all the products/services list out all you'd like to offer. Again, keep it simple if you are just starting out. Each one of these boxes is like starting a small business. Writing and promoting a book – small business. Keynote and workshops – small business. So try to work on one revenue stream at a time so that you give it the concentration required to Launch successfully.

Be sure to fill in your income goals and you can even work backwards from that goal to figure out how you are going to get there. Over time this model is going to evolve and change and you'll decide which aspects of the business you love more than others.

You'll probably look at some of the examples and revenue numbers in this book and think they are unattainable, but let me reassure you that every speaker, no matter how successful, started with zero engagements on their calendar at one point in time. Allow yourself to dream, to shoot for just a little more than you think is possible. Stretch!

Bob Parker never imagined that his life would include trekking race cars around North America, but check out his Flashpoint for inspiration on what's possible.

BOB PARKER

Pit Crew Challenge – Adopting a Business Model Like No Other

We all know the easiest way to differentiate yourself in the marketplace is, of course, to just be different. However, I learned it is not just in what you say, but it includes how you convey your entire message.

In 2001, I had a client who wanted me to share the concepts of high performing teams and do it in a memorable way, where people could effectively see the ideas put into practice. We know that a lesson discovered is a lesson learned, and when people discover the message themselves, it resonates with them for the rest of their lives.

From here, the Pit Crew Challenge was born.

An experiential learning activity where we use the metaphor of a race car pit crew to teach the concepts of teaming and collaboration. Participants actually change tires on a real race car. From this starting point, they build upon the lessons that are derived from trial, error, coaching, and their ultimate success. It serves as a practical platform to offer meaningful insights that can be implemented immediately to test the result.

The stories that people remember the most are the ones in which they have a role. In the Pit Crew Challenge, we make the learner part of the story, and then they tell it to others. What could be more powerful than that?

The result has had a positive impact on the thinking of leaders in global organizations from middle management right up to the executive team in a variety of industries and sectors. We've established meaningful partnerships with some of the top ranked executive education organizations in the world putting us in front of influential organizations to change the way they see learning and engagement.

The program went viral in 2002, but it had a different meaning way back then, and for us it still does: have race car and will travel. We've been all over North America teaching with the cars, with the odd guest appearance abroad, and we celebrate over 20,000 alumni through this once-in-a-lifetime learning experience.

How do you want your business to look?

How do you want to be spending your time?

Start-Up Speaker's Quiz

Starting up a speaking business is the same as starting any business. So you must do your homework and prepare. Worksheet 6 contains some questions that will allow you to assess where you are in the process. If this quiz *scares the pants off you,* good! The speaking industry needs committed people who are in it for the right reasons. If you are unsure or uncommitted, then you must reconsider. You need to do more work before you start or perhaps you might re-evaluate.

The speaking industry needs committed people who are in it for the right reasons. If you are unsure or uncommitted, then you must reconsider.

START-UP SPEAKER'S QUIZ

Ask yourself the following questions and answer with complete honesty. After all, if you can't be honest with yourself, who can you be honest with?

1. What do I know about this business? Have I done my research? What do I need to learn? (*Note:* This book is a good start!)

2. Is there a demand for what I offer? How many speakers are making a living doing something similar?

3. How much cash do I have set aside to launch my business? (This is a business; businesses require cash flow.)

4. Can I support a negative cash flow? For how many months?

5. Is this really what I want? Am I all in – 100%? (*Note:* You can still have a day job and be "all in" just treat it like a business, not a hobby.)

6. Is my speech prepared? Do I know the return on investment for the audience? Do I know what problem I'm solving?

7. Do I have the support I need to build this business (e.g., childcare, financial)?

8. Do I know who my competition is?

9. How am I, or how is my message, different from that of my competition?

10. Am I good enough to go the distance? Have people from within the industry (and people who could hire me) told me that?

11. Am I an entrepreneur? Do I know how to run a business?

12. Do I have a solid business plan?

13. Will my banker and my accountant agree that I have a solid business plan?

14. Is my topic relevant and timely?

15. How much do I know about technology and can I learn what I need to know?

16. Am I prepared, and have I freed up some time, to take consistent action?

If you answered negatively or were unsure about the majority of these questions, you might have some homework to do prior to starting this process. You might even decide that you don't want to move ahead. But if you answered positively to the majority, then we are ready to proceed. But don't think the tough questions are over – there are lots more where these came from.

Several people have written to me over the years asking if I would send them a free copy of my book. And, sometimes I have sent one, hoping to give them a leg up. But the most recent request came from someone who didn't have a credit card or a computer and couldn't afford a $20 book. I wondered, "How exactly does a person hope to start a business without any of the fundamentals?" This is a small business; you've got to have cash flow and tools to launch it. If you need to wait a bit to get some of your ducks in a row, then take that time.

How to Spend Your Time, Energy, and Money

Throughout this book you will find tons of ideas for things you should be doing – from developing the speech, to building marketing materials, to setting and raising fees, to working with bureaus, to hiring staff, to setting up your office with systems, to developing product. Yikes! That could be overwhelming no matter what stage of your career you are in. Stop and take a good look at Worksheet 7. No matter where you are in your career, you'll get some clarity around where you should best spend your time and resources. This should take off some pressure to do everything today!

FOCUS AREAS

BONUS DOWNLOAD

New Speakers • *0–3 Years*

- ☐ Follow the Ready, Aim, Launch recipe (see Chapter 3)
- ☐ Concentrate on making the speech epic (For more on this check out my book *The Epic Keynote*.)
- ☐ Position in the market as an expert
- ☐ Build marketing materials that represent you – they may not be perfect
- ☐ Create your social media presence and platform, with intention
- ☐ Develop relationships with clients – getting your name out there
- ☐ Pull people into your team who might help you get there (part time, virtual)

Intermediate Speakers • *4–6 Years*

- [ ] Add to what you have created – be sure to subtract what no longer serves you (if you just keep adding it will become overwhelming)
- [ ] The Speech – keep working it!
- [ ] Narrow your focus and/or niche market
- [ ] Streamline your website to remove outdated programs/offerings – don't just add, subtract
- [ ] Take your marketing to the next level (now it needs to be good)
- [ ] Reinvent/Reposition if necessary
- [ ] Continue to grow your social media platform and ensure you are converting some "likes" to clients (Narrow your focus if you are spread too thin.)
- [ ] Raise your fees
- [ ] Introduce a new product?
- [ ] Develop systems in your office – you'll need them now
- [ ] Build the team (staff – part time or full time) and make inroads with speakers' bureaus (Work the business yourself for a few years before doing this.)

Mature Speakers • *7+ Years*

- [ ] Reinvent and streamline
- [ ] Marketing and social media – get more focused, don't get complacent
- [ ] Reinvent/Reposition if necessary – new products, new offerings – stay relevant
- [ ] Subtract – audition all of your content to see what stays and what goes, same with target markets, keep things fresh for yourself
- [ ] Add something that excites you – keep your name out there in fresh ways
- [ ] Tweak your team/systems – by now your office should run like a well-oiled *machine*

You'll notice that we talked about subtracting from your business on several occasions within the Focus Areas. It's important as you grow to really evaluate what stays and what goes. Think of it like a packed closet. If you buy a new piece of clothing, you have to get rid of something old.

I've seen it time and time again where speakers just keep adding and adding (whether it be products and services, speech titles, etc.) and their business becomes cumbersome and overwhelming. I've experienced it in my own business. So be sure to do a full audit on your offerings and your website on an annual basis. "Out with the old" will become a good motto.

The Basics: Setting Up a Speaker's Office

Set-Up Checklist

Really take a look at all of the traditional things required to run a business and ask yourself, "Do I really need this?" Perhaps you won't ever need a piece of formal letterhead? Perhaps you don't need to establish a second landline for your phone – maybe a Skype phone number or your cell will suffice? Do people send faxes anymore? That might be one you can do away with too. This is your business. Set it up based on what's current and what's perfect for you.

Look at all of the traditional things required to run a business and ask yourself, "Do I really need this?"

With technology these days, a business can be run from a cell phone. If this idea appeals to you, try to keep your paper files to a minimum. Scan, e-Sign, and e-mail agreements. Use online stamps or a courier account rather than a mailing machine (for book sales). Keep your calendar on the cloud rather than on the wall.

That said, all of these ideas are options and you'll make your decisions based on what's perfect for you. I love the visual of a wall calendar, but I have never used letterhead and I haven't handed out a business card in years. But perhaps you plan to be out networking, so you may prefer to hand out business cards.

CHECKLIST FOR SETTING UP YOUR OFFICE

Here's a checklist of things you will need to get your business off the ground. Refer back to the explanations in the text if you need more direction.

- ☐ Company Name/Logo
- ☐ URL – secure www domain for website
- ☐ Business Cards (I haven't given one away in years but I used them a lot in the early days)
- ☐ Letterhead (you may be able to go without)
- ☐ Website/Blog

Social Media (I recommend using your own name whenever possible unless you plan on building a company you can sell)

- ☐ LinkedIn Account
- ☐ Facebook Account (if you are okay with a max of 5,000 friends, opt out of the Business Page where you have to "pay to play")
- ☐ Other social media (Instagram, TikTok, YouTube, etc.)

Office Set-Up

- ☐ Dedicated Phone Line (cell phone? Skype line?)
- ☐ Mailing Station (if you ship a lot of books, perhaps you buy postage online in the early days)

Equipment

- ☐ Computer (Laptop)
- ☐ Printer/Scanner/Fax (will you need a fax?)
- ☐ Clicker – remote control to change slides
- ☐ Accounting System Software (keep your books on the cloud so your team can gain access)
- ☐ File Drawers/File Folders (if I were starting up today, I'd go 80% paperless)
- ☐ 12-Month Wall Calendar (if you are visual, like me)

Administration

- ☐ Business License
- ☐ Tax Number
- ☐ Speaker Agreement (see Chapter 14)
- ☐ Business Bank Accounts – keep separate from personal, this is important
- ☐ Credit Cards – separate for business

Virtual Presentations (may not be needed right away)

- ☐ Stand-up Desk (optional)
- ☐ Ring Light (LED)
- ☐ Quality Microphone (e.g., Yeti)
- ☐ Switcher (you may go without)
- ☐ Virtual background (a great space is ideal (most authentic), but in a pinch Amazon has some cool virtual backdrops and green screen options continue to improve)

You'll want to budget for a logo (LogoTournament or Upwork can usually provide good options for reasonable prices). Don't spend a fortune with your local printer on business cards, when VistaPrint can serve your needs at a fraction of the price. Don't get lured into the higher volumes for a lower price per piece; 250 cards are plenty to get you started. You might change things up after a year or two of testing.

See Neen James's Flashpoint below and know that this story is aspirational and will help you envision your future business. Her business is over twenty years old, so some of these aspects, like team, may not apply to you today. But perhaps you can have this much sooner in your career with some careful planning? Wouldn't it be amazing to run your office from your phone?

As with many of the ideas in this book, take what you want and leave the rest.

That said, this idea won't be for everyone. As with many of the ideas in this book, take what you want and leave the rest.

NEEN JAMES

Running Your Business from Your Cell Phone

After thirteen years as my assistant, I read the words, "Please accept my resignation." Shock, disappointment, sadness, and then relief were the emotions I felt. Yet, it was the push I needed. We already had a ridiculously systemized office, but I knew there was so much more to learn, organize, and achieve in my speaking practice.

Evolution sneaks up on you ands, when she does, pay attention.

That resignation allowed me to evolve our systems, change our processes, and create a lifestyle I'd dreamed of, including the flexibility to travel for pleasure (no need for an office or large team), simply by choosing to run everything from my cell phone!

There was an unwritten rule in the speaking industry about needing to be a weary road warrior, constantly running from hotels, airports, and convention centers all while trying to accomplish business development, speech preparation, juggling personal and professional relationships ... and often being exhausted! I didn't want that anymore, so decided to do something different.

We would continue to delight our clients and business partners, and leverage technology with an incredibly talented team. I could be on a boat, plane, or an exotic international hotel and keep every project and presentation moving forward.

The convenience of carrying my office in my hand allowed me to connect directly with clients and manage multiple profit centers (speaking, consulting, and coaching), and location and time zones became irrelevant.

I was even more diligent with my calendar and establishing boundaries, offering a variety of scheduling links for appointments, and we designed more sophisticated systems, purchased software, and revised workflows. And I love it!

If you want to run your business from your cell phone consider these factors.

- Build a talented virtual team
- Systemize every aspect of your speaking business
- Provide options for your clients to connect with you
- Go paperless where possible
- Create boundaries for work, home, and your team
- Allocate days in your calendar for specific activities
- Take administration and paperwork on the road and then discard when actioned
- Conduct business development calls while traveling
- Leverage cloud-based platforms
- Use tools that sync with your cell (e.g., Google Gmail, calendar, drive, docs, sheets) and workflow and accounting programs (e.g., 17Hats and QuickBooks)
- Publish your preferred method of communication to everyone
- Use your "Out of Office" message creatively every day
- Meet regularly with your team (I suggest weekly one-on-ones)

Those are some terrific takeaways from Neen James. And when you communicate with her, more often than not, you'll see an auto response e-mail that starts with "G'Day" as she builds her fun Aussie brand into everything that she does – even her out of office notice. Consider what kind of vibe you want to give off when communicating with your clients. And please beware of the comparison game on all of these flashpoints. Neen is several decades into this business. Don't compare your year one to her year twenty.

Coach's Question

How can I make this journey as easy on myself as possible?

Now, Neen's story is one way of looking at your business, maybe it can help you shave a few years of trial and error off yours. Perhaps you go digital right from the jump?

Check out Julie Henry's journey for what happens when big-time life changes get in the way of all of your beautiful plans – and how to get your mojo back after losing yourself.

JULIE HENRY

Finding Your Own Way in Speaking

I've been a speaker for as long as I can remember. In the beginning it was easy – not necessarily the mechanics and I certainly had to learn how to talk to crowds of hundreds, then thousands of people – but when your subject matter is giant squid and tiger sharks, you'd have to work hard *not* to catch people's attention.

I was working in zoos and aquariums so as part of my job on an average day I could be found taking adults on a hike through the woods, teaching students about sloths before we slept overnight in the zoo, or entertaining 1,000+ people as they waited for the dolphin show to begin. And at every aquarium and zoo I worked, I championed the idea of designing leadership training and team-building retreats for corporate clients and was always excited when I got the chance to deliver these programs.

In 2008, I left this exhilarating (yet comfortable) world and started my own business. Suddenly without a world-famous zoo or aquarium in my title or a brand to which I belonged, I struggled on how to represent myself. Clients who would have jumped at the chance to work with me before, now questioned who I was, the depth of my experience, and if I knew what I was talking about. I cycled through four different company names, three different business partners, and two corporate structures. What was once seamlessly easy to me and irresistibly magnetic to audiences – stories and learnings from animals – had become a liability.

I was expressly not hired for projects or speaking opportunities because I had "too much zoo and aquarium experience" so I started to hide this part. I instead described myself as having experience working for both nonprofit and Fortune 100 companies (all true), which led to a complete distillation of who I honestly was in both my professional and personal life. I became a generic version, another "consultant" or "leadership speaker," complete with suits I never felt comfortable wearing and a briefcase I hated carrying. Personally, this artificial sanitation of who I was and what I cared about weighed deeply on my soul and ate away at my confidence.

When I look back on this part of my journey, I can see glimpses of my true purpose and impact trying to erupt repeatedly; every year, I would write and rewrite the same mission in some shape or form. I wanted to help people drive and survive change – and I wanted to do this by using animals as both the hook to get people interested and the teaching tool to help them retain and apply the information.

Then in 2016 I first connected with Jane, who became instrumental as my coach, helping me reframe my business in a way that was genuinely me. She helped me settle on the business brand, Finish Line Leadership, that I still use today and lay the foundation of how to market my services to solve business problems and what fees I could, and should, be charging. For the first time, I had a *business* coach who could help me build the business to support the life I wanted to live.

Then in 2018, my husband died. He had been battling cancer for more than five years and now I had two children at home – nine and ten – to raise on my own. While I had had years anticipating how my personal life would change, I was completely unprepared for how my professional life immediately became unmoored. Not only had he worked with me in an aquarium, then alongside me in my business, he had been my greatest champion. He was interwoven into every single facet of my business from the structured systems I had in place (influenced by his data-driven mindset) to the stories I told to connect with audiences and teach my techniques.

Each time I went to speak – whether it was a keynote address or an hours-long workshop – I would feel my guard go up as I was surrounded by minefields of memories. Panic attacks started occurring regularly and I literally did not know if speaking would (or could) be a part of my career anymore.

It has taken me over four years to arrive at a new, admittedly fragile, point. There has been no magic formula, no process that worked better than the others. It is a continual journey of trying, crashing, weeping, and rebuilding over and over again while giving myself plenty of grace along the way. In telling stories to my audiences, I've worked hard to figure out how I can honor him and our shared love of wildlife and wild places without setting myself up for a possible panic attack mid-speech or unnecessarily distracting the audience by taking them down the cancer and/or widowhood track. Everyone has their own story, their own trauma, their own triggers, and it has been vitally important to me to figure out how to stay true to myself while staying on message.

What really happened is that things unexpectedly shifted and I think these can be lessons for anyone starting down the road of speaking or finding themselves at a crossroad.

- I was ready to make my own mistakes. I wanted to own my imperfections and reclaim my joy.

- I wasn't afraid anymore of having my keynote not land right or whether or not a client could afford my fee. I stopped wishing everyone would "like me" and decided that each time I spoke I was there for *someone* – not *everyone* – but for that person(s), I was going to show up and give them all I had.

- I talked with a mentor about who I really was – a person deeply passionate about using animals as a way to teach people about change, teamwork, and resilience. I simply couldn't ignore this part of me anymore, and as it bubbled away during our conversation, he interrupted me and told me that these ideas I'd had for so long belonged in a book.

- I hired Jane (a second time) as my coach, as I knew I could not put a book out into the world without fully leveraging its impact for both my business and my audiences. She immediately understood my vision, pushed me in necessary (even though at times uncomfortable) directions, and was relentless in her support of me and what she knew I could achieve.

> Ultimately, it was this. During a conversation with a dearly loved friend earlier this year, he proclaimed, "Julie, you have nothing to prove anymore."
>
> Which I've now loosely (but appropriately) translated into, "I will embrace a fuck it mentality."
>
> And in our final coaching call for this cycle, even Jane remarked how different I seemed and how proud she was of my journey.
>
> When I exhale into the moment, I can channel that original ease that I felt early on in my career. When I lean in and let the animals help audiences learn about change, I can feel a sense of purpose again and know I'm making a difference. If you know me, you would know that the "friend" that shows up often in my stories is really my husband. But I can finally smile when I tell these stories – because he lives on each time I do. And when I let my reclaimed joy shine through, people respond.

I appreciate Julie being so real with us about her experience. There's so much to unpack there. It's hard for people to admit that things have been difficult and I think her story is one that allows you permission (from the get-go) to carve out your own path. I hope it will give you the confidence to stand tall in knowing that you don't have to be all things to all people, nor does everyone have to like you. And when life gets difficult, as it will, be sure to give yourself the time and grace to reinvent your new normal.

So you've got a vision for your future. You know the mindset required to get there. And you've seen what it takes to have success. Are you Ready? Cause this is where we expand the recipe. We've laid out the foundation and now we can dive right in. Come on, let's go get Ready!!!

Ingredient

I

READY

5

Positioning

Focus on Topic and Audience

The first ingredient in the Wealthy Speaker Recipe enables the speaker to focus on getting Ready and the value you bring to the table. You'll gain clarity on which topic area you want to speak on and who is going to hire you. Then we'll start the process for you to become an authority in this area and position yourself as the expert.

Although the speech is essential – we call it your most important form of marketing – we'll leave that to Ingredient II, Aim, as we'll be talking all things marketing in that section.

The first, and most important step, is picking a lane – the topic that you want to focus on.

Pick a Lane

Imagine you are a decision-maker (someone who hires speakers) and you are looking for a speaker to talk about leading an inclusive culture. You start looking online and you find a few speakers who cover culture plus several other topics. Then someone recommends a speaker who wrote the book on this exact subject and only speaks on culture.

Who would you pick? The jack of all trades or the master of one? You want to hire the best!

As a Wealthy Speaker, you want to be *that* expert, the best – the one meeting planners call upon for a speech on that topic. So you need to focus your attention and talents on one topic area. My friend Joe Calloway calls this "picking a lane" and takes this topic even deeper with his book, *Becoming a Category of One.*

One of my clients, Greg Schinkel, had been building a training company for more than ten years. They did corporate training on several topics and he was hired to do the occasional keynote. Greg came to me with the goal to expand his keynote speaking business but we ended up going far beyond that.

Greg's company had become the jack of all trades and the master of none – they provided training on managerial skills, sales, customer service, time management, etc. After crunching the numbers, Greg decided to drop many of his less profitable training courses and focus solely on what he did best, leadership. He had already written a book on leadership and had the expertise to back it up.

Almost immediately Greg's business shifted and he started doing more leadership training. Greg's profits also rose. He was no longer trying to please everyone and it was a huge relief. He trimmed his staff, offering his people contract work instead of full-time employment, and he moved his office into his home, cutting his overhead in half. Even Greg's health improved as the stress of running the training company was alleviated.

Stop spinning your wheels. Focus your time, energy, and resources on one area of expertise.

In the first year, they were more profitable than in the entire ten-year history of the company. The minute Greg stopped spinning his wheels trying to please everyone and focused his time, energy, and resources on one area of expertise, business started to flood in the door.

When I look back at Greg's progress, it amazes me what a change in focus, and going deep into one target market and/or area of expertise can do for a speaker.

Changing or Narrowing Lanes

Even the more experienced speaker may find a change is needed. Maybe the 200th delivery of the same speech becomes unsatisfying or perhaps your business growth curve has leveled out. Whatever the circumstance, it is important to focus on the new topic – signal and change lanes. Or perhaps you just need to tweak your existing lane to breathe new energy into it or even narrow your lane to solve one problem. Sometimes moving to a new level means being brave. Don't get stuck doing things you are good at especially if they don't pay well.

Watching Greg Schinkel go from a bunch of topics to leadership was a huge step. But when he focused more intently on frontline leadership in manufacturing his business skyrocketed (more on Greg's fine tuning in Finding Your Niche, below). Now, the majority of his big contracts remained in the training space, and you might not want to go there. Regardless, it's clear to me that going narrow on your lane can pay huge dividends in keynotes or training if you are brave enough to make the leap.

So how do you pick a lane or change lanes? The Focus Form in Worksheet 9 will help you pick a lane. Ultimately, our goal is to come to a crossroad where passion and profits meet.

Ultimately, our goal is to come to a crossroad where passion and profits meet.

FOCUS FORM

A good speaker can talk on a variety of topics, but a Wealthy Speaker focuses on one topic, solving one problem, possibly with more than one speech (all linking back to the same lane) – under the same umbrella. If you want to be the recognized expert – the one that decision-makers call upon when they need a speaker on that topic – you need to bring all your skill and energy to that topic. You must pick a lane.

Focus Form

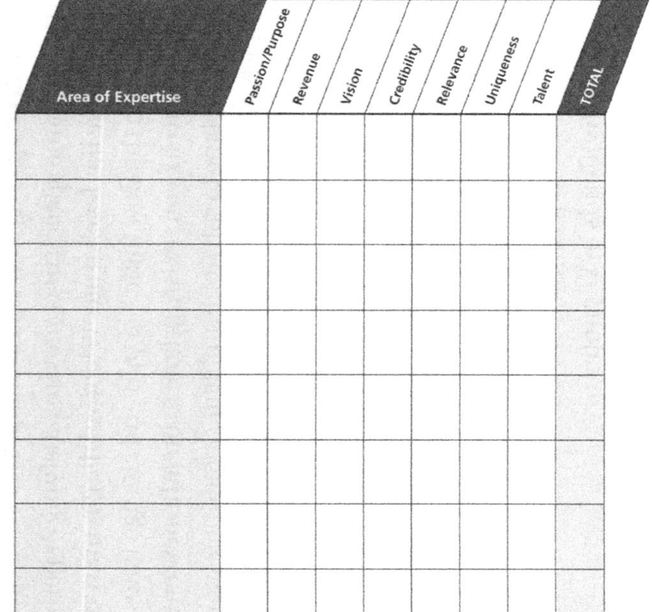

Area of Expertise	Passion/Purpose	Revenue	Vision	Credibility	Relevance	Uniqueness	Talent	TOTAL

STEP 1: List all of your speech ideas (things you could talk about) down the left-hand side.

STEP 2: Rate each of your speeches on a scale of 1 to 10—10 being a perfect fit with the criteria listed across the top.

Here are some questions to ask yourself when rating the criteria below:

Passion: How passionate am I about this project?
Is it in line with what I'm meant to do in this world?

Revenue: Is it a high revenue generator (8) or low (2)?
Who will pay to hear this message? (This one is key!)

Vision: Does it fit with my long-term business vision?
Can I see myself loving this topic in five years?
Is it an area into which I want to immerse myself?

Credibility: Does it fit with my background and credibility?
Am I walking my talk of this topic?

Relevance: Is the message timely and relevant for the audience?

Uniqueness: Is my message or delivery unique?

Talent: Am I really great at this?

STEP 3: Add the totals across and you should see which speech makes the most sense to proceed with. This is your lane!

wealthyspeakerschool.com

Which Audiences Will Pay?

Who is going to pay me is one of the questions that comes up frequently inside The Wealthy Speaker School. And it's a good question to be asking yourself. You'll want to figure out how to wrap what you know, your expertise, around an audience that can afford you.

Many speakers will pretty much stay open to all audiences for the first few years of their business, and then narrow to some focus niches later on. And that's perfectly okay. Marilyn Sherman, who wrote the Foreword for this book, has a terrific niche with women in food service, but she also speaks to many other audiences. Figure out one or two target markets that can give your outreach more focus, but remember that doesn't mean you won't accept gigs outside those niches.

Figure out one or two target markets that can give your outreach more focus. But that doesn't mean you won't accept gigs outside those niches.

Start with "what problem do I help solve?" using the Focus Form (Worksheet 9) to narrow down your ideas, and then move on to step two which is "who needs this?"

Being specific about your target market or focus is always the way to go. That doesn't mean you won't try some things that will fail and then move on to new ideas, but you want to be focused in your tests. Choose a target market that matches the following criteria.

1. What industries need your message?
2. What industries can afford you?
3. What groups of people are you passionate about and enjoy presenting to?

If you speak on leadership, for example, you might focus on these questions.

- Do I want to work with small business owners or corporate leaders (C-Suite)?
- Do I want gender-specific audiences (i.e., women only) or all audiences?

- Do I want to define my target market as business owners? From there you would want to find associations that cater to business owners (National Association of Small Business Owners), or if you want to target women (National Association of Women Business Owners). Please note, we will likely see more associations with a business slant popping up to accommodate LGBTQ so, although I may focus on some examples of women serving women's associations, I recognize that times are changing.

On the other hand, you may decide that your topic is on the lighter side, like building resilience through laughter. You could offer this up to anyone that might suffer from stress or burnout, perhaps industries that are "helping hands" types, like teachers or nurses. In this case, you will research what associations nurses or teachers belong to.

If you speak on sales, do you want to help small business owners or large corporate sales audiences with your message? Again, if you decide on one of these groups, you'll likely start to reach out to associations that house these people. If you wanted to focus on insurance sales people, you might find local, state/provincial, or national insurance brokers or sales associations.

Perhaps you speak on being your most authentic self. Our Mastermind member Heather Whelpley speaks on letting go of "perfect" and creating your own rules. She found an audience with women who work in typically male-oriented professions. Although she speaks a lot outside that audience, it gave her focus early on, and today her business is going gangbusters.

Another student, Chidi Iwuchukwu, wrote a book that helps people who are new to a country settle in and be productive. "But, how will I get paid?" he asked when first coming to our school. We talked about DEIB (Diversity, Equity, Inclusion and Belonging) being a current topic and how "belonging" is a big part of it. It was suggested that employers who wanted to hire people who are new to a country (in this case Canada) might need him. They might find his knowledge could help all employees in a company feel a sense of belonging. This started him down a path to explore whether or not he had a market with corporate in the area of belonging and potential paid speaking. It may be the perfect fit, or he may need to try another avenue, only time and testing will tell.

HOW TO SEARCH FOR PAID EVENTS

BONUS DOWNLOAD

THE WEALTHY SPEAKER SCHOOL
Build The Speaking Business of Your Dreams

How to Search for Paid Events

Let's break one industry down really far! Remember every one of these groups has an association.

- ☐ **Health Care**
  - ☐ nurses
  - ☐ nurse managers
  - ☐ personal support workers
  - ☐ administrators
  - ☐ social workers
  - ☐ kinesiologists
  - ☐ physiotherapists
  - ☐ occupational therapists
  - ☐ doctors (all specialties)
  - ☐ family physicians
  - ☐ health care assistants
  - ☐ nurse scheduling and support workers
  - ☐ audiologists
  - ☐ radiologists
  - ☐ personal care
  - ☐ rehabilitation consultants
- ☐ **Pharmaceutical**
  - ☐ sales
  - ☐ leaders
  - ☐ C-suite
  - ☐ customer events

ASSOCIATIONS	
Local	✗
State/Provincial	$
Regional	$$
National	$$$
International	$$$

CORPORATE	
National Meetings	$$$
Customer Events	$$
Regional Meetings	$$
Local Meetings	$

Topic Specific Conferences
- ☐ Safety
- ☐ Innovation
- ☐ Health/ Wellness
- ☐ Womens
- ☐ Technology
- ☐ Meetings Industry
- ☐ Travel

- ☐ **Education**
  - ☐ teachers
  - ☐ principals
  - ☐ teachers aids
  - ☐ superintendents
  - ☐ education administrators
- ☐ **Construction**
- ☐ **Hospitality**
  - ☐ hotels
  - ☐ restaurants
  - ☐ tourism boards
  - ☐ destination management

- ☐ **Automotive**
  - ☐ dealerships
  - ☐ aftermarket
  - ☐ owners
  - ☐ manufacturing
- ☐ **Technology**
  - ☐ users groups
  - ☐ corporate conferences

- ☐ **Financial Services**
  - ☐ Banking
  - ☐ Credit Unions
  - ☐ Finance
  - ☐ Real Estate
  - ☐ Insurance
  - ☐ Mortgage Brokers
  - ☐ Wealth Advisors

- ☐ **Retail**
  - ☐ sales
  - ☐ leaders managers
  - ☐ owners
- ☐ **Luxury Travel**
  - ☐ owners
  - ☐ operators
- ☐ **Franchise**
- ☐ **Transportation**
- ☐ **Agriculture**
- ☐ **Utilities**

- ☐ **Direct Selling**
  - ☐ corporate conferences
  - ☐ downline events
- ☐ **Non Profit** *(don't let the name fool you)*
  - ☐ volunteer events
  - ☐ fundraisers
- ☐ **Government**
  - ☐ front line
  - ☐ leaders
  - ☐ meeting planners (SGMP)
- ☐ **Speakers Bureaus (IASB)**

MY TOP 3 MARKETS

____

____

____

wealthyspeakerschool.com

Sometimes you may plan your market and sometimes your market finds you. You may not lock down one or two markets until you've been speaking for a while, but we do recommend that you have some focus when Launching your speaking business (see more on this in Chapter 10, Launch Strategies – Big Picture). Otherwise, you might just be throwing spaghetti at the wall to see what sticks.

Check out Worksheet 10, How to Search for Paid Events, and identify two or three target markets that might need what you have. You'll notice on the worksheet that we have also identified what types of events result in higher paychecks. *Note:* We borrowed some of these worksheets from The Wealthy Speaker School – just to give you a sample of what types of tools we provide there. (The goal is to make you curious. Did it work?)

Finding Your Niche

One of the major benefits of having a niche (an audience or industry that is the right fit) is that it gives you focus. Niche marketing allows you to develop a strong presence within a field. Then when you Launch, or relaunch, yourself, you know exactly where to start and who to contact. Without a niche, you're just throwing darts blind-folded, hoping you hit the target. That may be okay for a short while, but it's not super strategic.

Let's say you want to speak on sales and you want to specialize in the pharmaceutical industry.[2] That helps you have more clarity when reaching out with your marketing, yes? And, a side benefit is that when someone has a need in pharma sales, you'll be top of mind.

My good friend Odell Bizell has created a strong business model around the college and university market. He speaks on diversity and communication and young audiences adore him. We did a Wealthy Speaker podcast together where he shared all of his insider secrets to getting booked in the college market. If this is an area that appeals to you, check out the link in the Bonus Download.

[2]Sidenote, make sure that your niche is an industry that aligns with your values. You might choose *not* to focus on pharmaceuticals if it's not a values match.

Once Greg Schinkel picked his lane and switched from several training topics to leadership training only, he saw his business scale. But he continued to narrow his lane, and he found his niche market.

GREG SCHINKEL

Going Deep into Your Lane

Greg saw an opportunity to focus on leadership and he took it, but he didn't stop there. When the manufacturing world came to him with their problem of frontline leaders and managers needing training – he jumped on it!

An employee on the floor of a manufacturing plant might do a good job, so they get a promotion to supervisor. But they don't have any leadership skills and typically there was no training program in place. This is where Greg's company was able to step in and fill a vacuum. They provided the training that would allow the plant to meet its numbers and have strong leaders all the way up and down the line. Once they realized Greg specialized in their arena, clients were willing to pay more for Greg's team to work with them. He was practically the only game in town.

By filling a need, Greg was awarded contract after contract for large-scale manufacturing companies – many of them high six and seven figures. And he wasn't doing all of the training himself! He educated a solid group of trainers who became his "road warriors" and helped to fulfill these contracts while managing the team from his home office.

After teetering on bankruptcy a decade earlier, Greg moved his business into a highly profitable state, by going deep into one niche. His larger clients started referring Greg's team to other large clients and those clients asked for training to be delivered in English, French, and Spanish. To further lock down the business, Greg's team delivers training in-person, virtually, and on-demand.

Mining Your Background

A few years back, I had a client who came out of the real estate industry. He had worked his way up to broker/owner and had some outstanding results. Locally he was known as a leader in the real estate space. When we first started talking, he wanted to speak on leadership to the corporate world, specifically C-Suite. As we continued to dig, and work through Worksheet 11 (in the next section), however, it made more sense to him to focus on what he knew best, which was real estate.

If you are having a hard time finding a niche, then take a look back over the last twenty groups to whom you have spoken. Start analyzing them through new eyes and ask some questions.

- Which of these groups did I love?
- Which of these groups loved me?
- Who did I impact the most?
- Who can I help most in the future?
- Which of the groups could afford me without struggle?
- Which groups hold the most opportunity for future speaking engagements?

Finding your niche can sometimes take months or even years. As I said, many speakers work for every group in every industry and that is perfectly acceptable. Often they will have moved in and around companies and industries simply because word of mouth spreads.

And when you are starting an outbound marketing campaign (in the Launch phase), it's best to have two-to-three niches in mind when rolling out. When you find an industry that's a terrific fit, you want to double down on your marketing to that industry. Again, focus is king!

When you find an industry that's a terrific fit, you want to double down on your marketing to that industry.

My client Fahd Alhattab started speaking right out of college. He began with student audiences and eventually graduated into corporate with his message of how to lead and manage younger generations. He niched down to high-tech start-ups and quickly gained traction.

Brilliant! Because when these companies grow so quickly, leadership training becomes essential. And as a young person himself, Fahd was a unicorn in the market who could offer a different angle on how to lead.

Becoming the Legitimate Expert

In his book *Outliers*, Malcolm Gladwell states that it takes 10,000 hours to develop an expertise. Although that's a lot of hours, I do believe that stating that you are the expert isn't enough; you have to *be* the expert. Don't forget, if you've worked in a field for twenty years, you've got those 10,000 hours. If you are at the beginning of your speaking career and haven't quite nailed your expertise, you might consider Worksheet 11. Sometimes we take our expertise for granted, so let's make sure we do some mining. And don't be afraid to ask others what you are really great at.

BUILDING ON YOUR EXPERTISE

BONUS DOWNLOAD

What do I need to do to establish myself as an expert in my market? Your answer might come in the form of a blog, podcast, YouTube Channel, guest blogging in trade publications, writing your book, etc. You want to publicly link your name with the topic. This approach will add to your credibility as an expert.

Brainstorm and make your list now.

1. ______________________________

2. ______________________________

3. ______________________________

4. ______________________________

5. ______________________________

____

____

6 ______________________________

____

____

7. ______________________________

____

____

8. ______________________________

____

____

Coach's Question

What have I done over and over in my life and career that may help define my expertise?

What if You're a Celebrity?

Whether you founded a successful company, wrote a bestselling book, have a national radio or TV show, won an Olympic medal, are an entertainer, actor or politician, decision-makers may want to book you to help fill seats or add caché to their event. In some cases, you might be more recognizable for your accomplishment, or the story around you, than for your name. Think: the women that spearheaded equal pay in soccer, the Olympian that came back from cancer to win Gold.

Even though you're probably being hired to put bums in seats, your clients still want to know that you'll do a good job from the platform. I would encourage you to work hard at giving a killer speech. Why?

Because word gets around with decision-makers. If you give a mediocre speech or are difficult to work with, your longevity in the industry will be much more limited. Why not blow their doors off and have them say, "Wow, I didn't expect Jane Doe celebrity to be such a fabulous speaker!"

Back when I represented Sugar Ray Leonard at the speakers' bureau, I encouraged him to craft a meaningful speech. Sure people really just wanted a photo op or maybe an autographed pair of boxing gloves, but when he gave a really memorable presentation, our clients were pleasantly surprised.

In terms of speech content, I've seen many celebrities make the mistake of trying to be a motivational speaker, using all of the "believe and you can achieve" jargon. But that's not what you're being paid to do. They can hear a book report from any speaker. Use your life story as a backdrop for the lessons you learned along the way and build from there. If you don't tell your personal story, then you are most likely missing the mark. The real trick is to take the lessons you learned and help the audience with their challenges. It's a rare celebrity who takes the time to get to know their audience. When you turn your story around and make it about them, you are gold.

A few years back I saw a famous singer/movie star speak at a big convention. He oozed talent and he had quite a personal story to tell, having come back from an accident that nearly killed him. I couldn't wait to hear it. But he got up on stage and started rattling off some motivational hoopla and I felt completely ripped off!

Some of you could get up on the stage and spit nickels and your audience would rave about it, but the people who write the checks are really the ones you need to impress. Not many people in your world are going to tell you the truth or what you need to hear. I'd encourage you to seek honest answers and feedback, rather than listening to your "fans" or the people on your payroll.

The bottom line is that, as a celebrity, you have a responsibility to your client and audience to show up present, humble, and with their needs in mind. Check your ego at the door and do more than expected. You'll be rewarded with a long-term, profitable speaking career.

Getting Clear on What You're Selling

You've picked your lane and you've established your expertise. Now you need to focus on how to present this package to the world. How do you make it clear who you are, what your brand stands for, and what problem you'll solve for your audience?

For some speakers who have been around a while and are just adding to their offerings, this may be the missing piece of the puzzle. You might be unclear on the one problem you help to solve. If you are not getting the amount of business you want, check in and make sure that the value you are bringing to the table is clear and front and center.

Worksheet 12, What Value Am I Bringing to the Table, will help you identify the benefits you bring to the industry and, more specifically, to your clients.

WHAT VALUE AM I BRINGING TO THE TABLE?

Spell out the expertise and value you bring to your clients and ensure it is conveyed on all your marketing materials.

Here are some questions to help you draw out the information.

1. What are the results of my presentations?

2. What am I doing for people? Allow yourself to really explore this question to understand the full value of your expertise.

3. What problem am I solving?

4. Who really needs this message?

5. What is most unique about me?

6. How am I credible to speak on this topic?

7. How do I best deliver my expertise (keynotes, training, webinars)?

The goal is that when there is a need in the market, you are the "go-to" person to be able to solve it. And that you've communicated clearly how you can help.

While I was training with the Life Coach School, I realized there are coaches standing by to solve every problem under the sun. If you are a practicing doctor who wants to lose weight, there's a coach for you. If you have just had a painful breakup – check out the breakup coach who promises "get over your ex in six months or less." There are coaches who specialize in just about everything, and that's why I believe speakers should stake their claim to fame (and expertise) as well. Being a generalist can keep you busy, but it may not get you to your financial goals.

One of the first steps towards communicating your expertise to your target audiences (or niche) is creating a strong promise statement. Let's explore what that might look like now.

Your Promise Statement

You might recall that in the opening pages of this book, I made a promise to you about building the speaking business of your dreams. The goal was to have you lean in and say, "Yes! I want that!" (You're this far into the book, so let's assume that it worked.)

Your promise statement is your big picture - one line - that shows the decision-maker the results of your expertise. It shows what problem you'll help solve. You might also hear it referred to as a USP - Unique Selling Proposition or Brand Promise. Examples might be "Turning Managers into Leaders," or "Leading Teams Through Change," or "Boosting Small Business Growth," etc.

My promise for Speaker Launcher, my coaching company, used to be "Catapult Your Speaking Business." But as we've evolved and started our School and Masterminds, we've changed to "Building the Speaking Business of Your Dreams" to accommodate the emphasis on the Wealthy Speaker lifestyle being choice driven.

We'll take clear over clever if it means getting the message out sooner.

The promise is one of the harder things to nail but if you can just state your outcome, and provide clarity to the prospect that will be a start. Sometimes people will struggle with this for months because they are trying to come up with something "clever" but please remember that we'll take *clear* over *clever* if it means getting the message out sooner.

To get to this one-sentence promise statement, answer the questions in the first part of Worksheet 13 and then complete the form to lock down your idea.

GETTING TO YOUR PROMISE STATEMENT

BONUS DOWNLOAD

The promise statement, used for marketing, explains the big picture or the problem that you help solve. It shows the prospect the results of your expertise. Examples might be "Embracing Your Unique Self," or "Leading Teams Through Chaos and Change," or "Financial Common Cents for Small Business," etc.

Our Mastermind member (and associate coach in the school), Marc Haine, speaks to the hospitality industry. After trying out a few options, Marc came up with his promise "Building Lasting Connections to Make You THE Brand of Choice." There is so much competition in hospitality that this makes perfect sense.

The steps and the sample below give you an idea of the process. In the end you should have a short, powerful phrase that sums up what you do and who you do it for. Here are the steps.

1. List all of the outcomes that take place as a result of your presentations.
2. Now that you have your list, ask the question, "If people do all of these things, what will they get?" Continue to ask until you have another list.
3. Take a look at the entire list, circle the best and most unique words, and try to sum it up in one sentence.

Your Promise Statement: Sample

Barbara speaks to managers of franchises (mostly restaurants) about building their teams. So, she lists all of the outcomes (ROI) that will result because of her presentation.

1. Managers communicate more clearly and intentionally with their teams.
2. Managers will attract, groom, and retain top talent.
3. Managers will ensure that customer experience goes beyond company standards consistently.

Now she looks at this list. If managers do all of the above, what will that give them? She could bat this around for a while, but one idea would be that managers lead better. Therefore the phrase might be "Turning Managers into Leaders." (Remember, clear over clever if need be.)

Then she needs to check in with the marketplace. She needs to ask clients (preferably franchise operators), "How would your organization be different if all managers, at every level, were better leaders?" If they respond, "That would be fantastic," then she knows she is onto something.

Your Promise Statement

1. List all of the outcomes that take place as a result of your presentations. What will change in the organization or individual as a result of being in your session?

2. Now that you have your list, ask the question, "If people do all of these things, what will they get?" Continue to ask until you have another list.

3. Take a look at the entire list, circle the best words, and try to sum it up in one sentence. Make sure that your promise statement is one that will appeal to meeting planners – something that makes them say, "Yes, we need that!"

Now, let's transfer these ideas to our Wealthy Speaker School "What's My Promise" worksheet. You may want to keep it handy as we'll need it again in the AIM section.

What's My Promise?

Anatomy of a strong Promise Statement:

- Focused on them
- Outcome oriented
- Short and sweet
- Tells what you do, who you do it for

$10 WORDS

Does this promise demonstrate the outcomes of my work?

☐ YES ☐ NO

NOTES

MY PROMISE STATEMENT

wealthyspeakerschool.com

Your Name or Your Brand

Branding has a pretty large scope. A company name, the mission, the vibe, the personality that you project on your website, how you deliver presentations, and even your company colors can technically all be a part of your brand.

For instance, one of our Mastermind members, Tom Guetzke, has a brand around happiness and you'll see him wearing fun orange glasses and bright colors. "Live Happy" is his brand and he shows up with the smile to match it. That's an example of full-on use of a brand, which may come to you later.

There are a lot of terrific brands in our industry. My client, Shola Kaye (from the UK), uses "From Empathy to Equity" as her brand and "Curiosity, Compassion and Communication for Happier Workplaces" as the promise. That seems to be working quite well, as her business is booming, but it might change as she evolves her work.

But for ease and simplicity, let's make sure you lock down the basics - your name and your promise. For instance, you don't need a "Live Happy" brand like Tom. When just starting out, Tom may have used something like, "Tom Guetzke, Happy Habits to Live Your Best Life." The important thing is that the client gets it.

One exception is if you are aiming towards having a company that is bigger than you, something that you could sell to someone else. If this is the case, you'll want a branded company name. In other cases you - yourself - may be the brand. Either way, we want to show the buyer what you are all about.

As for a URL (your website address) if you don't plan to sell your company, I typically recommend going with yourname.com as it's the least likely thing to change. Often a speaker starts out speaking on one topic area but evolves into others. Using your name gives you freedom to evolve your topics without having to ever change your URL.

6

Fees

How Much Should I Charge?

When you are in the early stages of your career, this question can be very confusing.

I've always said that $1500 is the fee that moves you into the "professional speaking" realm. That gives you a number to begin with. But that's really just a number, it doesn't mean you can't charge $500 as a start. I mean, think about it, how many people earn $500 for just one hour of their time? That's pretty darn amazing, don't you think?

Consider that clients are not just paying for that one hour of your time, but the years of experience and knowledge that go into your expertise.

However, consider that clients are not just paying for that one hour of your time, but the years of experience and knowledge that go into your expertise. Many people are out in the workforce gaining knowledge for ten or twenty years before they deliver one keynote. The client is paying for two things – your unique perspective on a topic and your delivery of that perspective.

Your content and your delivery style will be what shoots your fee up the ladder quickly. I've seen speakers with very basic content (spun in an interesting manner) go extremely far in this industry because of their style.

One of our students, Emily Gower, wrote this Facebook post about why speakers charge what they do. I asked her if we could use it and she agreed. What a beautiful representation of what goes into one speech.

EMILY GOWER

Why Speakers Charge More

I had a valuable epiphany after my gig on Sunday about *why* speakers are paid so highly for their presentations.

It's not just the hour or so that we're on stage. It's all the pre-work. The clarity of the message. The development of the content. The generation of an original approach. The personal growth work. The work on developing confidence. The hundreds of talks to get ready for the next talk. The years of industry experience. The years of personal experience.

The preparation of the "runsheet," the slides, the jokes, the key points. The speaker agreements. The connection with the event organizer. The logistics. The choosing of an outfit (yeah, it's a thing). The travel to the venue. Taking care of our health beforehand so we can show up and shine.

And then when we're on stage, we manage *many* things at once, for that precious time we're with the audience: tone of voice, body language, posture, the energy of the room, the AV, microphones, responses of audiences, technology, slides, the "pause" (in speech), the timing of the talk, effective delivery of content, gauging what needs to be improved, inviting laughter, holding the space, sharing openly, being vulnerable (personal) and strong at the same time, use of the body – and more.

That is why speakers earn $1,000s or $10,000s for a talk. It's the ultimate pursuit of self and professional mastery. There is an enormous amount of love and persistence and devotion that goes into each talk – the readiness and the ability to deliver that talk *and* make an impact. ❤

One of my mentors (who just got paid $60,000 USD for a 60-minute keynote!) said recently that, "The ability to educate, inform, inspire and move people is one of the most highly valued skills in the world."

I feel it.

It's our destiny. It's why we do what we do. And it's why we deserve every single dollar that we earn along the way – and then some.

Tips on Setting and Raising Fees

Assigning a dollar value to yourself is not an easy task. Many factors come into play - some relevant and some not. Below are some pointers for setting fees and knowing when and how to raise them.

- Start somewhere (e.g., $1500). Do your homework, ask clients and other speakers for advice, and set a fee. It may be low to begin, but there's only one way to go - Up! You can raise it as you build your confidence and momentum.
- If you have any level of celebrity status - you have a successful podcast, are an influencer, wrote a book that's gotten some attention, etc. - then you can start higher than average. If you've come out of a high-level corporate position, that may also put you at a higher starting position.
- Put your fees down on paper in the form of a fee schedule and post it on your bulletin board in your office. Don't pull a different number out of the air every time a client calls. If you do seminars as well as keynotes, have those fees listed on the page. You may use this internally in the beginning, but eventually you'll want to make a fee schedule available for your clients or bureaus upon request. Everything that the client will need to set a budget should go on this page - include such items as speaking fees, travel expenses, AV requirements, etc.
- Don't post your fee schedule on your website. You want to have an opportunity to establish value with your clients long before the fee is discussed. Some speakers will only show numbers in proposals - never sharing the fee schedule and that is likely the way to go.

- Never charge more than your fee just because you think a client has more money. If you want to capture more of their budget, do it with additional value – coaching, access to your course or product – but keep your fee integrity.
- Travel expenses are typically separate from the fee. It's getting more and more common that speakers offer a flat fee for travel. The benefit of a flat fee is that the client is never surprised. You don't want your last communication with your client to be negative due to an issue with travel expenses.
- Test your fee with the people who book you the most (i.e., bureaus, clients).
- Harry Beckwith in "Selling the Invisible" talks about meeting a little fee resistance. If you are not meeting any resistance at all, your fee may be too low.
- Make sure that you are always giving more value than your fee. Your client should feel more than satisfied.
- Know what's going on in the market. Don't be afraid to ask people what they charge. It might surprise you. A great place to research fees is at eSpeakers.com. They have a fee range for each speaker.

A great place to research fees is at eSpeakers.com. They have a fee range for each speaker.

BONUS DOWNLOAD

When Should I Raise My Fees?

A great way to gauge if you are Ready to raise your fees is when these situations arise:

- Your clients tell you that you are too inexpensive or your calendar is getting full;
- You just released a new book or product that gains attention;
- You're often sharing the stage with much higher priced speakers; or
- Perception is hurting you.

Perception might be getting in the way of you getting booked, so be aware! If your fee is too low, you might be perceived to *not* be as good as you are.

Again, ask for advice from other speakers and clients and make sure you're not charging too little.

Don't allow fear to dictate your decisions. When you raise your fee, be prepared to lose 25% of your business from the bottom end, but know that you should gain 25% better clients at the top. Make room for those better clients in your business.

Fees Are a State of Mind

Fees are a state of mind. When a client calls you, is your negative thinking/thought (your inside voice) running the show or are you?

Either you believe – inside and out – that you are worth your fee or you don't. Has this conversation ever taken place for you?

> **Client:** I'd like to book you.
>
> **You:** Great! *(Inside voice/thought: "I wonder if they can afford me?")*
>
> **Client:** What do you charge?
>
> **You:** $5,000 *(Inside voice/thought: "Geez, they're never going to pay that much!")*
>
> **Client:** Can we negotiate?
>
> **You:** Well, uh, maybe ...

Of course they are going to negotiate. Your inside voice, your negative thought, is running the show! I'll say it again. Fees are a state of mind. When you first establish value and stand tall in your fees and state them with confidence, then people are less likely to try to negotiate. Now, there's the odd person that just has to ask for a deal, but for most, this is true. Here's how the conversation should go.

> **Client:** I'd like to book you; how much do you charge?
>
> **You:** Well, I'm not sure that I'm a fit for you. First, tell me a little about where you need help.
>
> **Client:** Our people are being asked to do more with less and they are starting to burn out.
>
> **You:** *(Inside voice: "I can help!!")* Great, I think I would be able to address that with my presentation called "XYZ." Some of the

benefits of XYZ are that your people will ... *(go on to describe the benefits and the return on investment).*

Client: That sounds like exactly what we need. What is your fee?

You: I charge $5,000 for a keynote and $6,500 if you add a breakout session the same day. *(Inside voice: "That's great value!!") Then you be quiet ... no if, ands, buts.*

Client: Great – I'll run that past my boss, Miss Jones, and get back to you.

You: In the meantime, let me send you an e-mail with more details, so you can review it and forward it on to Miss Jones too.

Did you see the difference? First we want to establish value, then we can talk fee. And most importantly, once you quote your fee, be quiet. If they come back to you with a counter-offer, then you would go to your list of reasons to negotiate your fee (see Negotiating Fees, below) and see if they qualify. If they don't, then be willing to give up that piece of business. You'd be surprised how often people will say no and then circle back to you later. They often find a way to make it work. You might offer to throw in some books or some other added value to help close a deal. But standing tall in your fees will serve you well.

You might offer to throw in some books or some other added value to help close a deal. But standing tall in your fees will serve you well.

Attracting Your Perfect Client

When I first got into the coaching field, I didn't know what to charge clients. I knew that my expertise was worth something, but I wasn't sure how much. I was trained at CTI (the Coaches Training Institute) and I heard a lot of fees mentioned – most of them I thought were extremely low. So I asked the instructor what fees he was charging. He was at the top of the industry, something like $350/hour. That was the figure I was shooting for, but I set my fee below his at first. I had to start somewhere.

Since then, I have quadrupled that fee, blew past the instructor, and it will continue to go up. I even raised my fees in the middle of COVID-19.

Why? Because I was due. Every time I raise my fees, I attract a more perfect group of clients.

But here's the funny thing. In the past several years, I can't remember one person asking to negotiate my fee. Why? Because my mind is not open to it. I don't make it an option. How could I possibly do that while I'm teaching others to stand tall in their fees? I'll talk more about attracting your perfect clients in Chapter 10, Your Perfect Customer.

Negotiating Fees

Write down specific reasons why you might negotiate your fee and tack them to your bulletin board. Then, stick with them. If a client does not meet your negotiation criteria, then you may decide to turn down the work. But please know it's your call either way. Here are some possible reasons to negotiate your fee.

- Multiple engagements (although if it means more work, I'd stick with full fee).
- Short turn around – the engagement is next week and local.
- Piggyback engagements – you are already in their city and can do more than one client in that period of time.
- They use you multiple times during their conference – many speakers offer a special price for a keynote plus a breakout in the same day – have a full-day fee on your fee schedule to inspire clients to use you more than once.
- It's a charity that you want to support (decide ahead of time how many per year).
- There's a major opportunity for book sales or some other back-end sale.
- It's an audience full of decision-makers, your perfect target audience.

Every meeting organizer will tell you that their engagement is *great exposure*. Don't take their word for it; do your homework on the group before you make the decision. Ask to talk to speakers they hired in years prior to see if the opportunity is as good as it sounds.

Being all over the place, or constantly negotiating fees, may bite you in the butt at some point. Many meeting planners will work with more than one speaker's bureau to find the speaker they need for an event. If two bureaus have submitted your name and if they are quoting two different fees then the situation could become sticky very quickly.

Bottom line about fees: Make sure that you are always giving more value than your fee. Don't be afraid to raise your fee; you may lose 25% of your low-paying clients but gain 25% better clients. Most importantly, negotiation is a state of mind.

ERIN DEIHL

Stop Chasing, Start Attracting

Have you ever known your own power, but tucked it away for a while? You know, placed it in a safe little drawer, and said "I'll see you when I do my spring cleaning … whenever that is."

For the first four years of my business, I attracted clients by referrals, networking, and the help of Google. We had a five-year growth plan for our business and were executing and crushing all of our goals.

All of this came to a complete halt in 2020, when in-person events ceased to exist, and my team and I decided to rebuild our brand and website. This meant an entirely different URL and all new SEO.

With the new way of conducting business plus a lack of leads, we did not see revenue for two-and-a-half months. Contract after contract was terminated, and I began to operate from a place of scarcity versus abundance.

I also got really close and comfy with my new frenemy, "comparisonitis." It stole almost all of my joy, and we had the low revenue to prove it.

In 2022, I decided to change my mindset, up level our offerings, and work with Jane. Within two sessions she helped me see the value of my time, and adjust our pricing accordingly, something my team and I had been working on pre-Pandemic, but forgot in the shuffle of the chaos. She helped me redefine the way I look at myself as a leader, and reminded me to take my power out of the drawer, and place it proudly in my pocket.

Within weeks, contracts started closing, leads poured in, and we started attracting more of our ideal clients.

As of today, my team and I just hit our end of year revenue goal – and it's only June! We've booked an opportunity in London, UK, and I'm stepping into my own as a keynote speaker.

I've got the momentum of Taylor Swift (how in the world did she create two albums in the Pandemic?!) mixed with the confidence of Beyoncé's *Sasha Fierce,* and I'm so ready for what's next.

It's all because I reclaimed my own power. The energy I'm emitting is magnetically attracting what we want – and my team and I are riding high from the buzz!

I've got the momentum of Taylor Swift mixed with the confidence of Beyoncé's ***Sasha Fierce.***

The Speaking World Pyramid

The graphic in Figure E will help you see how, as a new speaker, you might start out working and will graduate from level to level. Some may start right at the bottom, at the Rubber Chicken stage, while others might launch straight into Making a Living. Everyone will move through the steps differently. One of my clients started in his first year at Making a Living and has already hit the Sweet Spot within three years. Sweet!

Rubber Chicken

The Rubber Chicken[3] circuit is where many speakers begin. These are the freebie speeches that you deliver in order to get your momentum rolling. It's also a great opportunity to practice your speech. This might

[3]Many moons ago, we called it the rubber chicken circuit because the hotel meeting rooms often served a chicken lunch – and it wasn't always good. Fortunately for you, hotel meals have taken a turn for the better. Bon appétit!

be your local associations, non-profits, and service clubs, like Lions Club. As I've said, some of you will never need to go this route. Just know it's an option.

If you know what industry you'd like to get in front of, you can do all of your freebies more strategically. Let's say you want to speak to insurance people. Then your pro-bono, or low-bono, gigs could be at the local insurance association chapters all around your state or province. Try to keep your freebies close to home unless it's an ideal audience.

BONUS DOWNLOAD

FIGURE E:
The Speaking World Pyramid

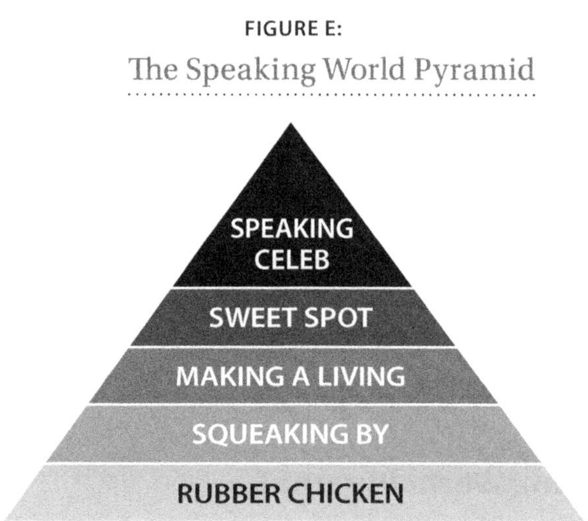

Squeaking By

A year or two into your business, you might be just barely cutting it. This is the Squeaking By phase. Your goal? To keep your momentum going and continue to raise your fees. You don't want to sit here too long or get stuck on the struggle bus. This is really the pay your dues period. Be conscious about whether or not you are getting paid what you are worth. Some speakers spend years in this phase and then give up. Your goal is to get really good and to ask for what you are worth.

I have a couple of clients who are in this phase right now. The hard work is happening during this period! But consider this, if you can get two-to-three spin-offs from every engagement in this first phase, then your marketing will get that much easier.

Making a Living

The Making a Living phase is a nicer phase to be in. You're paying your bills, you are comfortable. Making a Living might be exactly where you want to be especially if you are balancing a family or taking care of elderly parents. However, if you feel that you are under-utilizing your potential, you might aim for The Sweet Spot!

The Sweet Spot

Ahhhh, The Sweet Spot! It even sounds great, doesn't it? This, I believe, is the ultimate for most speakers. You're earning a way-above-average income, you're living the lifestyle of your dreams, and you've got money for a rainy day. The Sweet Spot allows you to retire in extreme comfort. Sweet Spot speakers sometimes get recognized at airports. Some of my clients are living the sweet spot – Meridith Ellliot Powell, Kendal Netmaker, Shola Kaye. The Sweet Spot is a brilliant place to be!

The Speaking Celeb

When you stop to think about it, we actually have quite a few people in our world who would be considered speaking celebrities. Some of my clients – Kindra Hall, Ryan Estis, Judi Holler – are either there or very close. That doesn't mean they are famous like George Clooney or Julia Roberts, but they have name recognition within the corporate and association worlds. There are some bestselling authors, like Simon Sinek, Brené Brown, and Mel Robbins, who also live in this space. Being a speaking celebrity means that you've got great buzz about your work, you charge more than $30K per speech, and you get recognized frequently at airports.

Bottom Line

With the on and off challenges of our economy, we need to be prepared to add more value without lowering our fees. Clients will appreciate someone who stands tall in their fees. Remember the old Dr. Phil line, "We teach people how to treat us."

Stand tall in your confidence, stand tall in your expertise, stand tall in your fees!

And when we set out to attract clients who are perfect for us, they'll see our value and be willing to pay. Stand tall in your confidence, stand tall in your expertise, stand tall in your fees!

I hope you'll find Judi's story aspirational. Really imagine yourself moving from one rung on the speaking ladder to the next. Remember, there are only two things you need to do to accomplish what she has done – mindset and consistent action.

JUDI HOLLER

Moving from Struggle to Sweet Spot

While I've never had any actual rubber chickens thrown at me, I've thrown many at myself. Meaning that no one could be any harder on me than I am on myself, and I have a hunch I'm not alone here.

I've had many bad speeches, outfits, hairstyles, and slide decks. But, I love them all because it shows progress, guts, and the beauty of transformation.

The rubber chicken circuit was the best for me because it was the beginning. This is when I started throwing rubber chickens at myself. I felt this meant I was doing it right! But, here's the thing, most people don't have the guts to start – to begin, and to, well, not be so great.

Once I toured the freebie circuit, I began to gain traction. I looked to baseball for an example. You need many "at bats" to perfect your swing and make it to the big leagues. I needed many stages to gain traction and get booked.

What helped me? A killer speech, confident delivery, a unique approach, preparation, and a deep understanding of my audience. I followed this formula and kept showing up, and, over time, I started getting paid for my speeches, and watched with delight as that fee went up.

I'll never forget my first standing ovation. Yet, don't let it fool you. One of my earliest speaking mentors once told me, "The standing ovations are great. The hugs, high fives, and selfies are great, but they are not the true sign of a good speech. You know you can make a living doing this and that you have a speech that makes an impact when someone comes up to you after your talk and says, 'I loved your talk, and I want to hire you for my event.'" That's one of my favorite parts – getting that "spin." That's how you know you've got something good.

Growing a seven-figure speaking business is something I'm insanely proud of and have worked my tail off for, but it's not what I consider the sweet spot, nor does it give me the feeling of "making it." Would you happen to know what does? Love.

I knew I hit my sweet spot when my self-trust, self-love, and mental wealth prioritized the outcome an audience, client, or person has to my work. Anything can happen at any time; none of us wake up with a script because life is improv. No matter what happens on stage, I know that when I get off the stage and lay my head on the pillow at night, I'm proud. Of myself. Of my work. Of my life. Of my talent. I know I'm doing work I love, the way I want, with people that rock, and is there anything sweeter than that?

Now that we have figured out what we are selling and who is going to buy from us, we've picked a lane and set some fees, we are Ready to move into marketing – the fun stuff! Let's go!!

Ingredient

AIM

7

It's All About Marketing

Taking the time with Ingredient I to focus on your positioning gets you *Ready* to take *Aim* at your marketing. Your marketing materials need to reflect the benefits of your presentation, tell what problem you will solve, and showcase your brand and personality. And remember, the best form of marketing is a great speech so we'll include that here as well.

Marketing Materials – What Do I Need Exactly?

The manner in which clients buy has changed over the years and will continue to change along with technology. The old method of marketing was called "call-send-call." You would call someone on the phone to see if they had a need. If they did, you would send them your marketing package that included a folder of print materials and a VHS (yes, that's how old I am!) demo video. After a week or two, you would call back to follow up.

Now with technology in place, you'll likely go about it very differently but the concept of call-send-call is still valid. You might send someone an e-mail query (see Chapter 12 for a discussion of How Else Can You Get Their Attention?) to establish whether or not there is a need for your topic. If you do call them, you might have them go to your website while on the phone, or you might send them an e-mail proposal once the phone call is complete. Ideally, of course, you want them to be calling you because you've established yourself as an expert or because they were referred to you by a colleague. With this said, you need to prepare for all occasions and give them sufficient tools to book you.

Ideally, of course, you want them to be calling you because you've established yourself as an expert or because they were referred to you by a colleague.

To market effectively, you want to Aim at four components.

- Social Media
- Epic Speech
- Website
- Video Samples

Your speech and website are very important elements of your marketing – they are vital for a Wealthy Speaker. Also, each of these pieces are composed of many considerations and steps. Your speech and website each take a great deal of time to perfect, so we will deal with them separately.

Whereas before our "speaker" positioning (i.e., hire me, I'm a speaker) was front and center, now we want to position as an expert (who happens to speak) and who can help you solve a problem.

One Sheets – Do You Need One?

For me, the one sheet is an old school marketing tool. Why? Because everything you could say on a one sheet, could be said on your website. If you ask any speaker who is earning a significant fee, they are likely not using a one sheet.

That said, I have heard that there are still a few industries that will ask for one sheets.

So let's say you decide that you want a one sheet for a specific use, such as an industry-specific outreach. If there is a true need for it, then do it and have it in PDF form only. Make it something that someone could print off easily (printer friendly) and take to help them at a meeting to where they are deciding on speakers. Perhaps you include a short bio (it should tell them "why you" and not someone else). You can also include your keynote/workshop options with short outlines.

I would not recommend creating this yourself unless you are a graphic designer. If the committee is comparing one sheets and yours is less professional, you may not compete.

From a marketing perspective, I love the idea of a postcard. When you write a new book, you could have extra covers printed with a blank back and you could mail a bunch to prospects. Don't you just love to get something in the mail with a scribbled note on it? That really doesn't happen much anymore.

Social Media

Do I Need to Do TikTok?

Most of you will have some sort of social media presence coming into speaking and our goal is to really give you food for thought on how to make it more focused.

Do you need to do TikTok? If the thought of TikTok or any other social media makes you queasy, then don't do it. We're in this for the long haul and we want to choose things that are going to be fun and easy to do.

You might be wondering, how much social media do I need to do? Or how much time will I need to spend. And for that I just have one piece of advice.

Be intentional.

Most people set about marketing themselves on social media without a lot of thought. Here are some questions to help guide you.

1. Where are "your people?" What social mediums do they consume? If they are business buyers, they are likely on LinkedIn.
2. What mediums do you love? Are you really good at and love video? Think YouTube, Instagram stories or reels, TikTok. If writing is your thing, perhaps using the Newsletter or article features on LinkedIn is for you. People who loved to talk joined Clubhouse in droves during the Pandemic.

3. How old are your buyers? If they are young, consider Instagram or TikTok or whatever is the newest hottest trend.
4. How often will you post? Let's decide ahead of time and block it off on your calendar.
5. Who do you want to *be* on social media? The contrarian? The good news spreader, the fun, light-hearted person, the serious business "here's some good intel" provider? Have a common thread to your posts.
6. How will you keep your message in line with your "lane?" Make sure that you are helping your followers connect the dots back to your expertise.
7. Who will you connect with? Perhaps you talk to friends and other speakers on Facebook and conduct all of your business on LinkedIn?
8. What hills will you die on? Decide ahead of time what causes or politics you will or will not delve into and know the consequences of thoughtless posts or comments. A client will go back through your social media footprint to see if there are any red flags. Be intentional!
9. How many social mediums will you take on? My suggestion is three at the most. Over here at The Wealthy Speaker School, we focus on LinkedIn, Facebook, and Instagram – all under my personal name. We dabble (poorly) in YouTube and we've deleted my Twitter account.
10. How much time will you spend each day/week? Perhaps you set a timer to avoid going down those pesky social media rabbit holes.

Business Accounts or Personal?

If you plan to grow beyond 5,000 friends on Facebook, you'll need a business page. But here's the rub, most business pages are "pay to play" so if you aren't spending any money to boost your posts, you are likely getting very few eyeballs on your content. The majority of speakers do quite well using only personal pages for most social media. Perhaps you'll want to continually scan your list for people you can drop to keep your list under the max.

What Name Should I Use?

It's my pet peeve when I have to try to figure out who I'm talking to on Instagram because they have their company name as a handle. If you aren't fully branded and known by that brand (i.e., Dr. Phil), then perhaps use your personal name instead of your brand name on social media.

By the time this book gets published, all of these ideas on social media could be obsolete. But my goal here is to have you decide ahead of time who you want to be on social media and how much time you will put into that.

How do I want to show up on social media?

Epic Speech

There is no better form of marketing than a great speech. No amount of marketing dollars, no gorgeous Instagram feed, no ultra-cool website can overcome a mediocre presentation. It's important, so speech will have its own separate section (see Chapter 8).

Website

Everything about marketing has changed. Yester-year we used mailing packets and one sheets, now we use websites as our primary marketing tool. As such, we'll cover the many aspects of your website in a separate chapter (see Chapter 9) - there is just so much to think about and include. It truly is vital to your Aim phase.

Demo Video

Unlike websites that are mostly for image - who you are and what you offer - the main use of your demo video is to secure bookings. It should demonstrate enough of your live speaking presentation to answer the question, "Why should I hire this speaker over all of the others?"

The goal of your video is to help you make it to the short list.

A client typically starts with ten or more ideas and then starts to narrow down to a short list. The goal of your video is to help you make it to the short list.

I believe that once you surpass $3,500-$5,000 in your fees, the video becomes an important decision-making tool the meeting planner will use. Picture a boardroom table with ten people sitting around it, viewing one video after another. They might be looking at your website at the same time. Chances are that the way they react to the video will ultimately be the deciding factor in whether they book you or another speaker. So let's build a video that *gets you that booking!*

When you are a known expert, you get into the boardroom competition less and less. One person decides that the company needs your services (hopefully the CEO of the company) and they hire you without considering other speakers. This is when you have moved from being a commodity speaker to an expert. This is the goal. Either way, the client will want to see that you can hold your own on the platform and an epic video will help close the deal.

Many executives or planners searching for a speaker are conducting web searches. That means that if they don't see what they want within the first few minutes on your home page, you may lose them. The best way to capture their attention so they'll look around is with a home page video. It's short, two or three minutes max, and it's not you talking to the camera about how to use your website. It's you speaking live (ideal) or talking about the work that you do (and the benefits to others). When someone wants to hire you to speak, they want to see you in action – first and foremost! Once again I'll refer you to Kindra Hall and Ryan Estis to see some stellar demo videos that work.

When someone wants to hire you to speak, they want to see you in action — first and foremost!

What Does a Captivating Demo Video Look Like?

Again, this may not be necessary, but if you really want to deliver a demo, here are the components to a successful video. The most important are discussed below.

- **Humor** – If you can make your viewing audience laugh within the first few seconds of your video, then your chances of getting booked go up. Let's go back to the scenario of a group of people watching video after video in the boardroom. Once everyone has laughed, the energy in the room changes and they relate that good feeling back to you. If you have humor in your speech, then use it, and use it up front. Put your best foot forward.

- **Energy** – The toughest thing to capture on film is what happened in the room on the day you shot your video. Audience reaction is key to getting good footage. You need at least a two-camera shoot to capture the audience's reaction. Ideally you want audience members laughing, crying, being engaged, or taking notes. Capturing them laughing or clapping is helpful, so make sure they are mic'd for sound.

- **Quality** – Before YouTube and Reels made three-minute videos so popular, the quality of the shoot was extremely important. Unless your brother-in-law is an experienced videographer, do not ask him to film your demo video on his iPhone (although it's crazy how far cell phone technology has come). The professionals know what they are doing. Camera angles are important, sound is important, even panning the audience takes technique. A homemade video looks like a homemade video. If you are after a quality demo, you need a quality shoot, done on quality equipment, by professionals. Avoid footage that is more than three years old – trust me, you've changed.

- **Audience** – Consider the type of audiences that you desire (500 people or 50 people) and then try to film that same type of venue. If you seek to speak to groups of 100 or more, yet have footage of 20 people on your video, you are shooting yourself in the foot (no pun intended). If you can't seem to secure big stage gigs, use the "will speak for video" approach and offer to do some big stage work at low, or no, fees in order to gain footage.

- **Patience** – No video is better than a bad video. Wait for the right opportunity to film. You need to be prepared to update your video every twelve-to-eighteen months, so know that your first video will not be your last. You don't want to spend a fortune. Your speech is going to change, evolve, and hopefully continue to get better over time and you always want to be prepared to have your video reflect that development. If you have been speaking only for a short while – *Wait.* Allow your speech to evolve for two years before going down the demo video path. You can be taping yourself (either audio or video) in order to improve the speech, but don't rush the demo video.

  When I arrived at Vince Poscente's office he had already started sending out a bad demo video to bureaus and clients. It took us years to undo the damage and start working with the bureaus and clients who had viewed that video. We also made the mistake of not putting his best stuff first. We thought it was so unusual that it would scare people. That decision was based on fear. As soon as we changed it, the bookings rolled in. See Vince's flashpoint, later in this Chapter, for more on this idea.

- **Crap Shoot** – It's almost always the most amazing presentations that you don't film – ask any speaker. It's a gamble. Make it a habit to ask clients if they would like to tape your presentation for their internal use. They often respond positively. You might even encourage it in your speaker agreement. You would just ask for a link to the video in return for allowing them to film you. If they decide to do a one-camera shoot, you may decide to pay for the second camera yourself. Larger conventions will often use a production company to handle all of the audio/video needs. Working with that same company can help make the filming of your presentation more seamless.

  It is wise to have your expectations in writing, so that you get what you want in your video footage. That way if the filming does not turn out, you have some recourse. They may do everything right and the footage still isn't satisfactory – you may have to try more than once to get great footage.

- **Brief** – Overall, it's my opinion that a three- to four-minute video is plenty. If I'm not sold in the first ninety seconds of your video, chances are good that I won't be sold in the twelfth minute either. That being said, I have heard some decision-makers say that they prefer a full-length tape. You should have both available – a full, unedited presentation and a demo video.

  If I'm not sold in the first ninety seconds of your video, chances are good that I won't be sold in the twelfth minute either.

  Speakers' Bureau owner Martin Perlmuter told me the story about viewing videos with a CEO client one day. He booted up the first video, the client watched one minute and then said, "Next." Martin thought, "Uh oh, this isn't going well." They went through five videos in under ten minutes. At the end, the CEO said, "I'll take that third speaker." Martin realized the client knew what he wanted and he wasn't wasting any time making a decision. It was all good!

- **Expertise** – Your video must demonstrate the fact that you are credible to deliver this message. It answers, "Why should I listen to you?" Some people establish credibility with the use of voice-over or some written commentary that tells people about you. Avoid cliché terms and anything that looks cheesy. If you have current TV footage of you being interviewed, you may want to include brief clips to add to the credibility factor and the personal touch. I love one-on-one videos where the speaker is talking about their expertise and how it helps people. You can also include some personal elements here.

- **Style** – What the meeting planner really wants to see is you speaking – your on-stage style. Avoid having five minutes of pre-amble before they see you speaking. Have your speaking clips available fairly close to the start of the video.

- **Answers the Question** – The bottom line is that your video answers the question, "Why should I hire this speaker?" Make sure that you do a trial run of your video on multiple clients or speakers' bureaus *before* the final edit to see if that question is being answered positively.
- **Tells a Story** – The masters level video tells a story that draws the audience in. Take a look at Video Narrative's portfolio for videos that tell a story and check out Chris West's master tip later in this Chapter – he is the brains behind Video Narrative.

VINCE POSCENTE

Getting that Epic Video

I recall coming onto the scene to work for Vince Poscente as his agent in Dallas many moons ago. Vince was "off the ground" as a speaker. He had scored some paying jobs and he was interested in expanding his bureau business.

Before I had arrived in Dallas, Vince had sent out what could only be described as a "mediocre" demo video to all the speakers' bureaus. Ooooops. Not the best first impression for sure and it took some time to overcome.

When working on the next version of the video, we had a lot to work with. In Vince's keynote opening he'd get up on a chair and demonstrate the sport of speed skiing in a very energized and off-the-chain manner. I was a bit worried about showing that up front in the video (a fear-based concern). I feared that the more conservative audiences wouldn't buy it. But once we made the decision to place his uniqueness (the chair) at the front end of the video – everything changed!

That was the video that speakers' bureaus took notice of, and that was the video that put Vince on the path to eighty gigs a year at a very healthy fee.

This next segment is a master's level tip, so if you are in the early stages of your speaking business, please know that this isn't essential for your first video coming out of the gate. Be patient, and know that this is the ultimate video concept that you can circle back to when ready.

CHRIS WEST

How to Master the Epic Video

The purpose of an effective speaker demo reel is to distinguish yourself in a crowded market and ensure you are placed on the short list among the thousands of other speakers available for that event.

For many years, a speaker demo reel followed the traditional approach of lining up speaking clips to "demonstrate" what you can do on stage. This is an appealing approach that many bureaus still love, and there is a place for a longer format video that shows only speaking clips.

However, in a crowded market that is growing every day, your primary speaker video needs to distinguish you and create a lasting emotional impact on the viewer. To achieve this outcome, you must take a narrative approach to your video.

The most effective narrative speaker demo reels progress through five movements.

Movement 1

Start with a story or question that distinguishes your personal brand. When a mind hears the beginning of a story, it needs to hear the end. When you ask a question your viewer has been asking themselves, their mind needs to know the answer. If you take one of these two approaches to the start of your speaker video, you will catch the viewer's attention faster and hold it for longer.

Movement 2

Next, provide insight into the greatest challenges your audiences face, so they know you understand their struggles and how to help solve them.

Movement 3

Once they know you understand them, share your backstory or show your credibility through graphic titles and images. Show them why you are uniquely qualified to help them solve their challenges.

Movement 4

Now you teach. You give specific tactical strategies they can apply to their business or personal lives. If you have a model for how they will experience transformation in their lives, this is the time to share it. Stay high-level and provide only an overview. They need to book the full keynote to get the content.

Movement 5

Finally, you show results and leave the viewer inspired by result-oriented speaking clips and social proof through written or video testimonials. This outcome is achieved best when you bounce back and forth between a speaking sound clip and social proof. This assures the event professionals they can expect similar results when they book you for their event.

When you know these movements and are intentional with the structure of your speaker demo reel, you will witness far greater consistency in your bookings and less resistance to higher fees.

8

The Epic Speech – Your Best Form of Marketing

We've placed this in the marketing section because – and you might get tired of hearing this – there is no better form of marketing than a great speech.

There is no better form of marketing than a great speech.

Your speech may already be developed or you may be starting from scratch. Either way, this section will help you design a speech that will blow them away every time.

To dive deeper on speech and presentation skills, check out my book *The Epic Keynote: Presentation Skills and Styles of Wealthy Speakers.*

BONUS DOWNLOAD

Although the majority of this information crosses over and can be used for training, breakouts, or workshops, in this section we are talking primarily about keynote presentations ranging from thirty to ninety minutes. To decide what forms your presentation will take, see Chapter 4, Getting Ready for Market.

Be Unforgettable

A great keynote speaker is someone who can keep an audience mesmerized for up to ninety minutes. With the success of TED Talks (typically eighteen minutes), shorter presentations are often being booked. An "epic" presentation might have people go through a series of emotions or take them on a dramatic journey. Some of the best speeches stay in your memory for years.

I still remember, 30+ years ago, Captain Jerry Coffee (who sadly passed away in 2021) spoke at my very first speakers' convention in Washington, DC. I can recall vividly his story of being captured and being held as a POW (prisoner of war) in Vietnam. He talked about how the prisoners in tiny 4 x 6 cells with dirt floors, developed a communication style between them. They used Morse Code to tap out messages to each other between the walls. In fact, I can still hear him using his hand to knock on the wood and how that echoed through the microphone. You could have heard a pin drop in that room of over a thousand speakers and there was not a dry eye in the house. The fact that I can remember this so vividly over three decades later, when I often can't recall why I walked into a room, tells me something. Captain Coffee was memorable and had impact!

Your speech is your best marketing tool, so let's make it epic - let's sharpen that saw! Here are a few coaching questions for you.

- What story will you tell in your speech that people will remember ten years from now? (Perhaps that becomes your "signature" story.)
- What feeling do you want people to walk away with? (Energized? Inspired?)
- How will you deliver your message in a unique manner?
- What phrase or common idea will glue your presentation together?
- How will you make it about them and not you?
- How can you craft the speech to have ebbs and flows?
- Will people be inspired to "take action" after listening? What do you want them to do?

What Makes a Great Speech?

Although I'm not a speech coach per se, I've helped many of my clients put together epic presentations. Here are some really basic takeaways to level up your speech.

- Speaking is a craft. So "winging it" is not an option. Write out your speech (or at least the key stories) and rehearse it. Know exactly how long it takes and be prepared to cut some of it when the meeting coordinator tells you, "We're running behind."
- Your keynote should have a beginning, a middle, and an end. And the opening and closing stories should be powerful and solid.
- Use plenty of stories to illustrate your points. Too much teaching and you'll lose your audience.
- Weave your energy throughout your presentation. Be conscious of when you have bursts of high energy (perhaps faster/louder) and when you are very calm and soothing to the audience. Energetically, it should be a roller coaster journey.
- Try to have the room set for success. This may look different for everyone, so here are a few considerations. Avoid dance floors; a huge gap between you and the audience will stunt your energy. Long, narrow rooms are tough; set them up sideways if possible so you are in the middle of the room with the audience huddled around you. Theater style seating is better than round tables, but I have seen many successful speakers in a luncheon format with huge audiences rock the room. Just know you have to work a little harder to keep the attention and the energy.
- Try to avoid distractions like food service. Ask the meeting coordinator to have coffee and dessert on the tables and all plates removed prior to you starting.

  Have something prepared for every awkward moment that could potentially occur (waiter drops a tray, cell phone rings, fire alarm goes off, medical emergency). Always be prepared.
- Use your voice, pitch, tone, and pacing to take your audience on a journey. Be intentional with how you use the stage as well. Avoid

Be intentional with how you use the stage. Avoid the pacing tiger.

the pacing tiger. Use the front center position as your power place for key moments and lines.

- Have one central message that ties the speech together. Stay focused on your message and your expertise. Avoid rants.
- Do your homework to ensure that you know your audience and how your material can be utilized in their lives. Many speakers use a pre-event questionnaire. You should be interviewing the client (and possibly several members of the audience) as part of your research. On top of your regular questions, you'll want to make sure you are asking the client "what would make my presentation a success in your eyes" and "how will you measure success." Check in with them close to the day of your speech as well. If you are speaking to a corporate or association market, then you must have your finger on the pulse of their business or their industry's. If the cover of the *Wall Street Journal* has a story about your client facing huge layoffs on the day of your speech, then you must be prepared.
- If you use PowerPoint or another slide program, use it as a visual aid, not a crutch. In a business presentation, the fewer slides the better. An inspirational presentation (someone who has climbed Everest) can be much more riveting with photos that help the audience feel like they are there with you. An oldie but goodie book that references PowerPoint is *The Presentation Secrets of Steve Jobs* by Carmine Gallo.

BONUS DOWNLOAD

- Allow your passion and enthusiasm for the topic to shine through. If it doesn't, then you may not be speaking on the right topic. Allow your values to guide you on this point and be brave when it comes to dropping a topic.
- Know your best audience size. Some people know that they really shine in front of a huge crowd, while others will do better with smaller audiences. There is a certain talent for reaching people in the far corner of a stadium of 15,000 – you either have that talent or you must learn it. Either way, know where you fit best.

- Arrive at the event early so that you can see what has gone on before your talk. You might get some material that ties in perfectly – and makes you the hero. It might also save you some embarrassment by not telling a story that's already been told.

- Use current references. Stories that worked ten years ago probably need to be changed or, better yet, tossed out. Keep an eye on the headlines for the timeliest stories. Trust in your ability to come up with new material and if you need help, then seek it out. Your audiences may see twenty or more speakers a year, so keep it fresh.

- Be relatable. One of my coaching clients is a multi-millionaire who started his business doing every job himself, including cleaning the toilets. He needs to have a mix of toilet stories that balance out his jet-set millionaire stories or the audience will not be able to relate to him.

- Make it about them! If you are new to this industry, then unfortunately you missed out on one of the best speakers of our era. His name was Art Berg and he passed away in 2002 at age thirty-nine. Art was a quadriplegic who told the story of how he came back from a paralyzing accident to live a "beyond full" life and excel at anything to which he put his mind. Art's theme was "while the difficult takes time, the impossible just takes a little longer." I saw him at a conference once and his career was catapulting. I asked him what he had changed to have so much success. And he said simply, "I made it about them." Sage advice for any speaker. No matter how the story or message is delivered – in Art's case the story of how his paralysis changed his life – you can always turn it around and make it about the audience, rather than yourself. (Fun fact, Art was also the Founder of eSpeakers, which we have referenced a few times in this book.)

- Be your authentic self. When you see other speakers present and admire their style, be careful not to copy. Being your most authentic self is key to the audience engaging with you. (See Shelley Brown's Flashpoint at the end of this list.)

- Make sure your introduction is solid, short and sweet, and sets you up as an expert. Tell the MC exactly how you would like it to sound (and name pronounced). Even though you will be asked for your introduction ahead of time, always carry a spare copy to events in case of emergencies.
- Create a phrase that glues your presentation together. (This is Master Speaker level.) A phrase that pays (thank you Doug Stevenson) is a very short sentence that you offer up to your audience at the beginning of the speech and then continuously sprinkle throughout the speech. At the end you drive the phrase home. Kent Julian has a throughline or "Phrase that Pays" for his student audiences, "Either stay home and whine or show up and shine." I'll bet that would look great on a t-shirt!

  The phrase should be short and meaningful. It should be something that people want to repeat to each other. If it drives the audience to action, then even better.

SHELLEY BROWN

Finding Your Uniqueness

I was raised in the corporate world when feelings were an "HR problem." I desperately wanted to express myself, yet I spent more time, effort, and struggle trying to fit in, a story that is all too familiar to many. My life was very compartmentalized. At work I felt like a human measurement as in KPIs, metrics, and data. In my personal life, I measured my self-worth by the numbers on the scale and the number of completed marathons as a way to deal with all of my overthinking, difficult emotions, and low self-esteem.

After suffering what I jokingly refer to as my nineteenth nervous breakdown – in all seriousness, complete amygdala hijack – I discovered the life-changing practice of mindfulness and made it my mission to become certified and educate people on this life-changing practice. I became a mindfulness educator and developed a program using rock music to teach mindfulness to the skeptics in the world from which I came, the corporate world where feelings were still an HR problem.

I had some great gigs with my speaking and workshops, and I was gaining traction but then the Pandemic hit. I had time to evaluate. I was being asked to speak virtually about mindfulness to provide folks some tips to help reduce the overwhelming stress people were feeling brought on by the world's events but I realized after doing a few of these events, it wasn't my lane.

I stopped speaking and instead focused on my art and writing my book, *Weird Girl Adventures*, a compilation of stories about the trials, tribulations, and triumphs of finding my way to embracing my own "weirdness."

Eureka! Writing the book made me realize my highest value is belonging! And mindfulness is really the foundation of our ability to amplify the experience for not only others, but for ourselves as well. I came up with a framework using the word W.E.I.R.D. Now more than ever, feeling weird is a universal experience in all areas of our lives and certainly in the context of work.

It took me a little bit of time and certainly some help to incorporate my storytelling, my quirky art, my book, and my mindfulness education as well as little bit of singing into my speaking, but as soon as I was able to be totally myself and communicate my value proposition authentically to address a universal struggle and position myself as a relatable, fun, storyteller, artist, speaker with a dose of some mindfulness gravitas, that's when my speaking business started to take off.

I was able to be totally myself and communicate my value proposition authentically.

I thought I needed to be some lofty, buttoned-up expert with a bunch of professional certifications after my name. But the reality is I just have to be me with the desire to use my voice to serve in a way that's entertaining, educational, and, most of all, authentic.

I love that Shelley, in the middle of a pandemic, stopped to ask, "How can I serve?" And she went on to create value for people who were feeling the same way she was in her job – underappreciated and not valued.

Belonging has become a hot topic in the corporate world, and I don't know that I see it going away any time soon. Well done Shelley for asking good questions.

How do I want to show up when I take to the stage?

This next section is all about moving from good to great in your presentation. If you are new to the business, review it now and circle back to this section once you have your foundations in place. Kelly Swanson has been wowing audiences for years and when it comes to stories and humor, she is the bomb!

KELLY SWANSON, CSP, Hall of Fame Speaker

Eight Tips to Create an Epic Keynote

I was so excited when Jane asked me to contribute to her book. She is amazing, and has helped so many speakers define their brand, their strategic plan, and execute it in a way that stands out from the competition. She asked me to share some tips for an epic keynote, and I want to note that I am laser focused on that word – *Epic*.

Plenty of people can give you tips on a good-enough keynote that does the job and communicates your ideas effectively. But I have spent my entire career looking for ways to do one better, to create a wow factor, to stand out among the competition, and to deliver something people have not seen before. And, yes, with good solid content and clever marketing behind it. That "one better" is what truly creates a different level of speaker. Because I believe there are no hard and fast rights and wrongs in this industry, and because I don't want to tell you how I do it, but rather encourage you to find out how *you* want to do it, I will phrase my tips as questions to ask yourself and explore. So let's jump beyond the expected and find out what lies in the category of an *epic* keynote.

1. **Good: A really strong idea.** Not just a bunch of tips cobbled together. But one really strong idea worth spreading. A philosophy that encompasses everything you teach and encourages them to change their perspective on the problem they have and the desire they seek. What is your idea worth spreading?

   Epic: Make it sound sexy. Different from anything they have heard before. Disrupt the status quo. Connect it to the hot topic of the day. Example: My program was first called "Hanging on to Humor" then I changed it to "Who Hijacked My Fairy Tale: Hanging on to humor when life doesn't go the way you planned." When I wanted to make it relevant to the client, I called it "Who Hijacked My Healthcare System."

2. **Good: Show them you *get* them.** Understand and illustrate what problems they have, how that's making them feel, what desires they have, and how that's making them feel. This isn't about what you think they need, or even the meeting planner. It's about tapping into *their* story. What motivates them? What does your audience care about? How do they know you *get* them?

   Epic: Instead of just telling them you know how they feel, show them. Find a way to *illustrate* life from where they sit. Example: When I want to illustrate how people self-sabotage with their inner script, I open the speech by talking to myself in a mirror.

3. **Good: A clear understanding of your style.** Are you lots of humor with a light relevant message? Are you deep content with a lot of interaction? Are you facilitating a group conversation with tips woven in? Do you play games and crack jokes? Are you taking a take-off-the-face-and-get-real approach to your subject? Are you touching and heartfelt? Are you a combination of Tony Robbins and Oprah? No matter what your topic, consider that you are the "artist" on that stage – your brand has a style. Understanding your style will keep you from reinventing the wheel every time you write a speech, and make it easier to sell, and more marketable if you show people what they will get. The style sets you apart from every other speaker.

Epic: Find a unique way to illustrate your style that is different from other speakers. Example: There are many examples of speakers who dress like their signature story in their keynote. The wingman dresses in his military uniform. The guy who went to prison does his speech wearing orange coveralls. The woman fighter pilot comes out wearing her flight suit, and then takes off the uniform to a suit underneath. One woman did a speech sitting on a tall ladder. One man did his speech sitting in a wingback chair. All of these decisions were in alignment with their brand and story, not just random decisions. I have a story about chub rub in sequin pants, and am considering wearing the pants in my keynote.

4. **Good: A clear understanding of your substance.** This is about your content. What solution are you selling to their problem? Whether it's one concept, or twenty, do you have a good grasp of your curriculum? Are they just random points you are making, or a clear path to a destination?

   Epic: Sell the transformation and end result. Wrap your curriculum/content/talking points into one bucket. A method. A system. A formula. Four steps to this. Five pillars to that. Don't sell all you know; sell the system you have created. People love to buy a system. Example: I used to tell people I would come teach them the power of story. Then I changed it to "I will come teach you my Story Formula which is a three-step system to take you from learning about emotional connection, to finding the story idea, to crafting it out, to powering it up."

5. **Good: Have a clear outline for your keynote** and a reason and purpose for everything. A strong open, a strong close, and variety. Do they walk away repeating key phrases from your speech? Were they given a clear action step? Did you create buy-in instead of just a data dump? Did you seed for other business? How do you want them to think and feel about you, the topic, and themselves, and does your speech do that?

   Epic: Don't just tell it – sell it. Create a solid persuasive speech structure that serves as your sales argument, that is more than an outline of your talking points, but a journey you take them on to get them from A to B. Just like the steps you take in a sales presentation. Even if your model is more of a relevant message than deep content, you can still persuade them. How are you at going from telling people what they should do to making them *want* to do it? How are you at getting their buy in – getting them to uncross their arms? Example: Go to www.KellysFreeGift.com and find the Story Lib Workbook. There is a Speech Structure Outline on the first page.

BONUS DOWNLOAD

6. **Good: Sell *you* just as much as your content.** Allow them to *get* you. Too many speakers simply share the information. We may love what we hear, and take great notes, but we walk away not remembering *you*. Telling them what to do is not the same as making them *want* to do it. If you can make your audience *want* to take action, you *will* get booked over and over and over. So you have to sell this, not just tell this. That makes you a salesperson. And the cardinal rule of sales is that people buy from people they like, trust, believe, and feel like they know. Stories are the only way to show people who you are without just telling them. Do you have a story that tells them what you care about? Are you showing them what this message/topic means to you personally? Do you share how you relate to the pain they have in a personal way?

   Epic: Find a creative way to tell them about yourself instead of just telling them about yourself. Example: I have a monologue of things I learned in 2020. It's funny. It tells them about me. And it spins into a poignant point about how I believe in silver linings.

7. **Good: Create an experience, not just a program.** It's the experience they buy. Focus on how to turn your content into an *experience*. What does that look like? What are the different ways that you can change the way a program looks and sounds and feels? Music? Lights? Interaction? Games? Videos? Where do you come from when introduced? Props? Act outs?

Epic: Do something they haven't seen before and come out of your comfort zone. For years, I taught people my Persuasion Principle concept in a very "teacher" way. Now I get people up on stage to play the Dating Game. It's a fun way to illustrate the teaching in an analogy they can all understand. Sometimes I will dress as the server and be pouring the water for my audience before I'm introduced, and then weave it into a message about leading with a servant's heart. The phone ringing from Prides Hollow is another example. These are the things people will keep talking about after the day is over.

8. **Good: Have an *amazing* STORY.** Someone once told me years ago that the best speakers are the ones with the best stories. I would tweak this to say that the best speakers are the ones with the *right* stories. I don't care what you speak about, or to whom, or how much content is in your program – the truth remains – *the story* does most of the work. Do you have stories that illustrate and put a human face on your talking points? Do you share examples of your content in action with a face and a name? Do you use stories as a strategic tool to make someone think, feel, or act a certain way, or are you just using stories because someone said you should? Do you wing your stories and settle for good enough? Do you ramble through your story? Do you understand the lesson of your story and state that clearly?

   Epic: Take your stories over the top in how you deliver them. Start a big story at the beginning of your keynote and finish it at the end. Weave a story all the way through your keynote. Have music play behind your story. Example: I once wrote a story about what a guy in a vacuum store taught me about customer service. The story was great. But I wanted to do one better. So I added music. That was great. But I wanted to do one better. So I hired someone to create a video of a hand drawing out the scenes of that story, and had that play beside me on the screen so that when I told the story, the hand drew it. That was pretty darn cool.

How Important Is It That the Speech Is Good?

We've said it before and we'll say it again: It's the only thing that matters. It's everything. No impressive website or flashy marketing can overcome a mediocre speech.

No impressive website or flashy marketing can overcome a mediocre speech.

"Be Good" Marketing: Spin-off Is King

There are really two types of speaker marketing. One I like to call "be good" marketing and the other includes the traditional types of marketing such as websites, videos, social media, etc.

Judi Holler started her business by doing all of the marketing things right – e-mails, phone calls, social media. And she got booked. Because she was fabulous from the platform, that turned into a very highly profitable spin-off business that has lasted for years.

Many speakers use evaluations and they average five smiley faces out of six. And people line up at the end of the program to say, "Thanks, that was awesome!"

A speaker friend of mine sat at the back of a meeting room waiting for his turn to speak. They were taking a short break and then the speaker before him would wrap up. He went into the washroom and heard two guys complaining that the material was fairly outdated and they weren't at all impressed. The meeting resumed and the speaker finished his talk. The two guys from the washroom were the first two in line to say to the speaker, "Hey, great job, thanks so much." So what does this tell us? Use evaluations and comments from the audience to build confidence, but do not take that to mean you are great and have no room for improvement. The number one way to know if you are really good is when people hand you their business

The number one way to know if you are really good is when people hand you their business card after the speech and say, "I've got a group that needs to hear that exact message."

card after the speech and say, "I've got a group that needs to hear that exact message."

If you are not getting an average of two or three spin-off gigs (additional pieces of business) from each speaking engagement, some exceptions apply, then you need to go back to work on the speech. Find yourself a speech coach, books, training, whatever it takes. Continually hone your speech and it will pay off for you in the ultimate reward of more engagements.

Check out my book, *The Epic Keynote*, for some great tips on speech and recommendations to several coaches.

LINDA EDGECOMBE

Humor = Spin-off Equation

I did not plan on being a professional speaker. I had a job that put me in front of lots of folks and that led me to being asked if I would come and speak at a few companies' staff days. I have always had an irreverent sense of humor. And it has served me well in the past thirty-plus years. So when BC Hydro asked me to come and speak at a staff Wellness Day I said yes. All I thought about was "I have no idea how to fill an hour. But if I get them laughing, they won't care."

I told a few of my mishaps and ideas about stress management and they laughed and booked me for most of the offices around the province. I just couldn't believe someone would pay me good money to speak to their staff. One of the best things I ever did was keep a journal of interesting things that happen to me every day. I would wind those experiences into stories to make a point about what I was talking about. I have never been afraid to embarrass myself or walk to the edge of what everyone thought and told me was appropriate.

All I knew was that the funnier I was, the more bookings I got. My goal from the start was, for every gig I attended I wanted two more engagements. That approach and mindset has been steadfast for thirty years now. I have to admit that for most of my career, I have always felt like I have never really "been discovered." I know that's my ego talking. And I have rarely asked for help, most likely out of insecurity.

But, as I have aged and gained wisdom, I have used every bit of "life" that's been dealt to me as content for my presentations. Because I know for a fact that most of my audiences are going through *stuff*, just like I am. So, I stand in very strong convictions when I deliver content that is real, raw, and refreshing. But I also know that my sweet spot is to surround everything I speak about with a ton of humor. That allows my audiences to relax into the truth of themselves. And it helps them retain the content longer. And because I get them laughing, I get tons of spin-off.

Here's to laughing more.

Industry Green Monsters: The Comparison Thief

Sometimes you might be sitting in an audience, seeing a speaker you've heard raves about, and think, "What's all the fuss about?" You think they are just okay. Or maybe when you read Linda's Flashpoint just now you felt the green monster of envy rising up.

Ask yourself this question, "Am I simply feeling jealous?" Believe me, it's common in this industry despite the fact that we are a group of highly evolved and well-adjusted individuals. People get jealous – no big deal.

And it's true. Please don't compare Linda's year thirty to your year one or two or wherever you are. Instead of leaning into the green monster, let's ask a few questions.

- What can I learn from this speaker?
- What is it about their style that gets them booked?
- How far along (years) are they in their business?
- What have they done differently?
- What are my next steps, and how can I focus on those?

Theodore Roosevelt once said, "Comparison is the thief of joy."

9

Crafting Your Website

Before we dive right into your website, let's get very clear on what you want this website to convey and how your personality is going to shine through.

Now, when you go to a professional agency like Chris West's Video Narrative or Azadeh's Gogo Telugo Creatives for branding and website design, you are going to go through a comprehensive, deep dive process starting with your vision and mission and moving all the way through to what you want your brand to stand for and how Search Engine Optimization (SEO) is going to drive and convert traffic. For the purpose of this book, we're going to give you the basic essentials.

Website Goals

Your first step is to really get clear on the goals for your website. What do you want to happen once people arrive? What's the call to action (CTA)? How are people going to find your website, what are you doing to drive traffic to it?

Your website is your first line of offense when it comes to marketing. It's your image, it's your giant calling card, it's a chance to really Wow! the client. With today's gorgeous templates, there is no reason not to have a beautiful (and updated) website. If your site is more than three years old, consider an update. If your website is homemade consider hiring a professional.

One of the key goals is that you are positioning yourself as an expert who can solve a problem versus the "hire me, I'm a speaker" approach.

Step 1: Focus Your Content

One of the most difficult tasks for a business owner is writing the copy (the content) on their website. The number one reason for this? Lack of clarity on the exact problem you are helping to solve. And perhaps not being crystal clear on who your market is (your avatar). It's especially difficult to write website copy when you are thinking about serving multiple markets. For example, a speaker might have one program for women in the food services industry and another completely different program for real estate people. That's going to make creating a website difficult.

My client, Moira Kucaba, recognized that in order to bring her website all together she had to bring a few ideas under one umbrella. As the top coach for Beach Body and a seven-figure earner, she wanted to keep her Rise Up Course, which helps women alter their lives and health, front and center. Through keynotes and workshops, Moira also wanted to help show other entrepreneurs how she made the big turnaround, from college dropout and addiction to self-made millionaire. And as a big-time social media influencer (over 100K followers), she would draw a crowd. So working with two audiences, we set about creating a website that had one message about transforming your life.

Sidenote about Moira's site: She was able to use some of her team to get the site 80% done and looking fabulous. But when they got close to launch, she needed a web professional to step in and ensure that all pages were viewing beautifully on desktop, laptop, and mobile devices.

You might do the same if you are using a template to build your first site. Get the content in place and then hire a designer to "make it pretty" for you! And before choosing which platform to use, make sure it's one that is supported by many. WordPress maintenance, for instance, is quite easy to come by.

Prior to getting started on your website, you'll want to consider these questions.

- Who is your avatar (a representation of your ideal customer)?
- What is your lane (your topic area/expertise)?
- Who are your target markets? Will you focus on a few industries or one?
- What vibe or flavor do you want your website visitors to feel?
- What call to action (CTA) will be sprinkled throughout?

We often get the question, should I write my copy for the audience or for the person writing the check. Let's use an example of someone who speaks on building high-performance teams. If you focus on copy that describes the outcomes of the work you do (stronger bonds, creative solutions, happier workplace), then you are really able to serve both the audience and the buyer.

Perhaps in website stage 1, you get the framework of the website up and running. Take the website quiz to ensure you are on track (Worksheet 14). Then, add more bells and whistles (videos, lead magnets, blog) in stage 2 or 3. Don't feel like you have to have everything ready before launch; this can progress in stages.

You also might circle back after your initial launch and ensure that you have all the things necessary for SEO. Let's get that Google juice flowing! We want a leg up anywhere we can get it, although you'll likely be the one that drives the majority of traffic to your site through your marketing.

Should I Put Fees on My Site?

What should not appear on your site can be as important as what should appear. I have just one item that should be avoided – fees. You want to talk to a client or prospect in person to get them excited about the idea of working with you. Never rely solely on technology to sell you. You want the opportunity to start to build a personal relationship. So always have fee conversations after you've established value and in person, rather than over e-mail, if possible.

Step 2: What Tabs to Include

The most common tabs or pages on a speaker's website are outlined below. As always, I encourage you to be unique, but don't be so "unique" with your tabs that people don't know what the heck you are talking about. Save your creativity for your website copy, but let your home page be called "Home" and your contact us page be "Contact Us." Don't make your clients guess at what you might mean with a clever tab title.

Further, I suggest keeping your tabs or pages to as few as possible. Remember a confused buyer doesn't buy. Here are your basics – in order and positioned top right of the page – that's where the brain goes.

Please avoid drop down lists – just let me go to the page and see what you have there.

Of course if you offer coaching, consulting, or a course, those might be tabs as well. And perhaps you don't have a podcast but you do have a blog, swap it out. Place the services you want to sell first immediately after the home page button. If speaking is your main goal, then it might go Home, Speaking, Coaching, and so on. And if you only want to speak, then Home, Speaking, About Us, Contact Us is all you need. Those are your mainstays.

My advice? Avoid drop down lists – just let me go to the page and see what you have there. The fewer choices to click from the home page the better.

Home Page Highlights

So, what are the key elements to include on your all-important home page?

- **Name (Logo):** The top left corner is typically the spot for your name or logo. You'd be surprised how often a speaker forgets to include their name.
- **Hero image:** This appears above the fold. This will be a photo that captures your essence, perhaps on a big stage if big stage

gigs are your goal. Above the fold means it's the first thing viewers will see on your website before scrolling. A moving image of you on stage looking animated is fine but not necessary. Your photos, in general, should allow the buyer to really get a feel for who you are, so sprinkle them throughout your site using a variety of professional and casual looks.

- **Promise statement:** Make certain this is front and center. It tells what problem you are going help solve (possibly who you solve it for).
- **Home page copy:** Talk about them and their problems, show them that you understand their pain.
- **Solution options:** Typically three boxes of how you can help - so if they don't choose a navigation tab, they'll see three ways for you to help. Keynotes, Workshops, Coaching, for instance, with a very brief (one line) description and link to more.
- **Clients' logos:** One line of logos on your home page showcasing your biggest and best clients. Testimonials can be sprinkled throughout, but make them short and sweet and focused on the outcomes of your work.
- **Calls to action:** Sprinkle these throughout. What do you want them to do? Book a discovery call perhaps?
- **Mini bio:** This should be very, very brief and lead to the About Us page for your full bio.
- **Unique factor:** Does the home page answer the question, how are you unique? Make sure they know all of the things that you bring to the table and why they should choose you as their speaker.

Now that we've covered your Home Page, let's give you the "highlights" for some of the other key pages - things to keep in mind as you are writing copy.

Speaking/Keynotes Page Highlights

The speaking or keynotes page is where buyers will go to see your list of topics and options. Let's not make them work too hard for it.

Rather than having ten reasons to hire you, just show me what your keynote speech options are – the program outlines. The format for the program outlines page could be as follows:

- Title,
- Subtitle,
- One paragraph that describes the program,
- Bullet points describing the benefits of that program (ROI),
- One short paragraph that describes your style in presenting the program, and
- A testimonial that backs up your style.

To differentiate your programs, you might add a little piece below the subtitle that describes the "Best Audience" and "Program Formats."

Here's an example.

> Leadership Communication: It's Not What You Say, It's How You Say It
> 45- to 90-minute keynote
> Best Audience: Leaders and Managers
> (Also available as a breakout session – up to 1 day)

Does the speaking page give your buyer one, two, or three options? More than three speech titles may confuse the buyer. Make sure your titles will draw them in and the subtitles really drive home what people will take away.

More than three speech titles may confuse the buyer.

Note: If you have ten options on your keynotes page, then circle back to Pick a Lane (Chapter 5) and narrow your ideas. A confused buyer never buys is the old saying. Less is more.

About Us Page Highlights

This is your credibility and bio page and can cover all of your achievements as well as some personal, fun stuff. If you can turn this page into a story, that will be helpful. Check out my bio. When you add some bullet points with your street cred, that allows the reader to get a feel for your story and hear why you are a good choice for them. Sprinkling in some fun facts (like where you live and who you live with, even pets) gives them some common ground to latch onto. "Oh, you have a labradoodle too!" "I used to live in Dallas."

Contact Us Page Highlights

This should typically be the last option on your menu or navigation bar. I recommend making it as easy and painless as possible for a client to get in contact with you. A decision-maker or bureau agent's pet peeve is not being able to easily find someone's e-mail and phone number on their site. Have your 1-800-number (or phone number) and e-mail address on every page if possible, and please don't ask the prospect to fill out a long form in order to make contact with you. It's okay to have a short form, just provide an e-mail address and phone number as well.

A decision-maker or bureau agent's pet peeve is not being able to easily find someone's e-mail and phone number on their site.

Should I Have a Meeting Planner's Page?

This page is typically where a buyer can get what they need once they have already booked you. This page might include your pre-program questionnaire, downloadable photos, bio (for publication), AV requirements, list of products and quantity pricing, articles that they can use before and after your presentation, and hand-out originals. Anything that a client might ask you for once a booking has been made.

You may not need a tab for this page. Make it *janedoe.com/meetingplanner* and give it to clients on an as needed basis. The meeting planner page becomes more necessary as you get busier speaking, so you might leave it off your website altogether when first starting out.

Rate Your Website

Once you've defined your website goals and built the appropriate pages, you need to step back and rate your site. Try to put yourself in your client's position and look at things objectively. You may want to run a beta test and get some input from people you trust. The main reason for having a website is to create an impression that will lead the prospect to think "this is my person." How well is your site doing this? Use the rating form in Worksheet 14 to set goals and make your changes in stages, if needed.

Bottom line: Your website needs to show me within ten seconds what you do and how you do it. So if I see your name, your brand, and promise immediately (i.e., above the fold), and then I see keynotes and workshops, consulting, coaching, bookstore, etc., in the navigation options, then I know what you do and how you deliver it. Make sense?

Note: If you include social media icons on your home page, you risk losing the visitor. It may still be something you want to do, but perhaps move them to your contact us page instead to lower the risk?

WEBSITE RATING FORM

BONUS DOWNLOAD

Rate yourself on a scale of 1 to 10 – 10 being perfect.

Many of these items will be found on your home page, but this references your entire website.

____ First Impression – does my website look professional?

____ Can the client easily determine what problem I solve within ten seconds?

____ Is my promise statement front and center?

____ Is my photography reflective of who I am? Is it creative or is it a boring head shot taken at Sears Portrait Studio?

____ Do I have a preview video that showcases my talent? (That may come later.)

____ Is my credibility present and clear?

____ Are my testimonials strong? Do they answer the question, "What changed as a result of my services?"

____ Are my client logos impressive?

____ Do I convey how I am unique?

____ Does the site reflect my personality, my values, and my essence?

____ Do I capture names and e-mail addresses effectively? (Lead Magnet)

____ Am I offering just a few places to click from my home page?

____ Are my tab names clear so that people know what I offer?

____ Do I have a strong call to action?

____ Is it simple for clients to get in touch with me?

Anything you rated six or less will need work in the future. Plan ahead and make the changes in stages if you feel overwhelmed. Go back and review the website section again if you need more direction on any of these items.

Coach's Question

How do I want people to respond when they see my website?

Would you like to see some websites that convey some of the features we've recommended? For many years we have run best website and best video contests and judged entries based on the criteria from this book. You can see the latest winners on our website. You'll find a link in the Bonus Download.

The next phase in the Wealthy Speaker Recipe is to roll-out to your market. If you've gotten *Ready,* taken *Aim,* then you're ready to *Launch.*

Ingredient

LAUNCH

10

Launch Strategies – Big Picture

Rolling Out to Your Market

Remember back in Chapter 5 when we talked about "Which Audiences Will Pay?" Have that target audience in mind when entering Launch. Launch is where the fun begins, because you are going to be talking to clients about booking you and getting paid!

There's nothing more fun than getting paid to speak.

I wonder how many of you were like me? Did you have a Mrs. Robinson in Kindergarten who wrote on your report card that you "talked too much in class?" Well, take that Mrs. Robinson – people now pay to hear what we have to say!

You're *Ready,* you've taken *Aim,* and now we *Launch!*

Accidental Versus Intentional Speaker

Launching your speaking business is like starting any business. It's going to take time and energy. But there are times when a speaker gets Launched inadvertently – they start getting asked to speak and it just happens without a lot of thought.

We call this "the accidental speaker."

Perhaps you scaled a mountain, won a gold medal or did something amazing that was speech worthy? (Hopefully you didn't have to cut off your arm with a pocket knife like Aaron Ralston.) Maybe you held an important job or wrote a book that's taken off? Or perhaps you delivered a Ted Talk that went viral or were a semi-finalist on *America's Got Talent*. All of these things are potential speaking career Launchers.

What we want to do now is move you from accidental speaker to intentional business owner. See the difference?

If you are not the accidental speaker, kudos because you've come into this with intention. Our next section is going to help you roll out to your target market.

As I said, one way that a speaker might get launched into the industry is through a Ted or TEDx Talk and Frank King has an interesting story on how that worked for him.

FRANK KING

A TED Talk to Reinvent

TRIGGER WARNING:
REFERENCES TO SUICIDE.

I was a writer for *The Tonight Show* for twenty years and a full-time comedian for thirty-five years. I have seven TEDx Talks, all on mental health, as I live with two mental illnesses, depression and chronic suicidal ideation.

I didn't choose suicide as a topic, it picked me.

It was April 10, 2010, when I came close enough to dying by suicide, that I can tell you what the barrel of my gun tastes like. Someone recently asked me, "What *did* it taste like?" I said simply, "Relief."

It was the height of the Great Recession, bookings for me, as a Corporate Comedian, dropped off 80%, and I was forced into a Chapter 7 Bankruptcy. My wife was devastated, which was devastating to me. As someone living with chronic suicidal ideation, I thought I had a solution for this. I had a $1M life insurance policy, and if I ended my life, my wife would be restored financially. Spoiler alert, I did not pull the trigger, but that's another story.

When speaking bookings did return, the meeting planners told me that the market would no longer bear a $5K keynote that was just comedy. They said, "You have to teach the audience something." I didn't think that I had anything to teach anyone.

Then a speaker friend recommended one of Jane's books. I went into it thinking that I had nothing. But with more thought, I realized that I did have something to share. I could "pick a lane." Given my close call with suicide, the fact that I live with mental illness – my family has more nuts than a squirrel feeder (I can say that because I'm one of them!) – I thought, "I can keynote on Suicide Prevention and Mental Health Awareness! That's my lane! I could become The Mental Health Comedian!

The only fly in the ointment was that I'd been a corporate comedian for twenty-five years. That's how the meeting planners and speakers' bureau people thought of me, as simply a funny speaker. I had to convince them that I could be a content speaker, who was also funny.

The solution? Do a TEDx Talk! I did that first TEDx (and six more) in my lane, Suicide Prevention and Mental Health Awareness, reinforcing the brand with each and every talk!

Ironically, coming that close to ending my life, revealed to me what I was supposed to be doing with my life. All of a sudden, I could see only one lane.

Not only did a TEDx Launch Frank's speaking business into a new topic area and lane, he's gone on to have a very successful speaking career on a topic that was quite a bit ahead of its time a decade ago. Today, mental health has become a topic that is gaining more and more attention every year. Just imagine how much companies are spending to keep their workers healthy? Why? Because it means less time lost

When you can tie your topic into a bottom-line-affecting issue for corporate, you are on to something!

at work, less health-care costs, less employee burnout. When you can tie your topic into a bottom-line-affecting issue for corporate, you are on to something!

A TEDx Talk is an awesome way to Launch a speaking career. So is writing a book. A lot of people ask, "What should I do first? A TEDx, write a book, or Launch my speaking?" The truth is it's been done in all ways imaginable and they all work. The best way to sell books is one audience at a time rather than one book at a time. But if you already have your book launched, this is good too. There is no one "right" way; the important thing is just to LAUNCH!!!

Planting Seeds: Work It Like a Farmer

Our best friends are farmers. And their business is input/output based. The more they plant, the more they yield. The speaking business is similar and even though we are not susceptible to all the farmers' woes, like bad weather, high seed costs, and shifting market prices, we have our share of challenges, like stock market meltdowns, pandemics, and recessions.

If you think about selling speeches like a blank farmer's field, it may help you create the vision. Each seed you plant (with a decision-maker), each time you pitch yourself, you have potential to see a harvest – a speaking gig.

But it doesn't typically happen after only one connection with a client, we have to nurture the relationship. Your initial contact with the client is the stage where you are planting the seeds. Plant enough seeds and you'll have a full calendar. It truly is a numbers game so consistency will be key.

Plant enough seeds and you'll have a full calendar. It truly is a numbers game so consistency will be key.

Next comes fertilization. I can see where some of you might think that you need to pile on the bulls**t here, but I mean rich fertilizer, something meaningful that you can send to the prospect to say "keep me top of mind" or "I have value for you." That might look like a video of your TED Talk, a copy of an article you just wrote, or a link to a podcast with you talking about solving a problem similar to theirs.

The follow-up is like the harvest. If you don't take your crop off the field and get it to market – what's the point? You have to follow up with every prospect that expresses interest and speakers who follow up consistently will see the pay day in terms of bookings.

When you have planted enough seeds, fertilized them (nurtured the prospect), and followed up with consistency, you will start to see your calendar filling up. But planting one row of seeds, and expecting a full bounty? That's probably not going to work.

Your Perfect Customer

Now I know this sounds a little odd to most people, but if you'll just give the process a chance you may be surprised. The book that I recommend to all of my clients on this topic is called *Attracting Perfect Customers: The Power of Strategic Synchronicity* by Stacy Hall and Jan Brogniez. Now, this book has been out for a while, so keep that in mind if you purchase.

BONUS DOWNLOAD

It leads you through a four-step process to attract the customers that you desire. I won't go into the entire book, but the first step is getting very clear on identifying your perfect customer. We could break that down even further to define who your perfect audience is as well. If you are just starting out in the speaking industry, you will need to go out and speak a lot before you will really know who is perfect for you. You might have to do a lot of speaking engagements that are not the perfect fit, before you can see clearly who is the best, most perfect audience.

Once you are clear, you can start drafting a list of the qualities of your perfect customer. As a coach, some of the traits of my perfect customers are as follows: they value my expertise, they can afford my fees, they show up on time and ready to work, they want to hear the truth.

As a speaker, your list might look something like this: they see me as the expert, as the solution to their problem; they pay me gladly and on time; they value my work and don't micromanage my presentations. Now is the time to start a list of the qualities of your perfect customer using Worksheet 15.

One of the steps in the attraction model is realizing what you need to improve in order to attract your perfect customers. One major step for new speakers is working on the speech. The attraction process will only work if the speech (your product) is Ready for the audience that you desire (see Chapter 5). In order to balance the attraction process, you need to ensure that you can manage the level of business that you want to attract.

QUALITIES OF YOUR PERFECT CUSTOMER

List the qualities of your perfect customer (including what their audience might look like).

1. ______________________________

____

____

2. ______________________________

____

____

3. ______________________________

____

____

4. ______________________________

____

____

5. ______________________________

____

____

6. ____

____

____

Your Targeted Approach: Starting Warm

When it comes to rolling out your business and telling everyone that you have something new to offer the world, you want to start warm and roll out from there. Your first stop (see Worksheet 16) is your inner circle, people who already know, like, and trust you. Perhaps it's people from your old job, family, friends, colleagues, peers. You might already have a fan base, perhaps you just didn't know it. These are the people you want to approach first to a) tell them what you are launching and b) see if they know anyone who could use your expertise. *Note:* You'll want to keep your e-mail short and sweet and reach out multiple times as people don't always hear the message the first time.

Next you'll reach out to warm leads. Perhaps you do a round of networking and start gathering up some warm leads so that the minute your website is ready, and you are set to Launch, you can put it in front of them. Some people will work the rubber chicken circuit (see Chapter 6) in order to have a list of warm leads. That's doing a series of free speeches in order to get your business Launched.

My first employer in the speaking industry, Betska (you'll read more about her in Chapter 12), did the rubber chicken circuit for three months prior to me going to work for her and it basically Launched her business. She spoke to any and all association and non-profit gatherings, including Rotary Clubs, and that was the beginning of a thriving calendar.

Once you have exhausted your inner circle and warm leads, you'll want to begin with target audience #1. This is where you'll need to decide who "your people" might be. Is it that insurance audience we discussed earlier? Or corporate? Or women's associations? You decide and move forward.

All of your ideas are going to be a test. If you reach out to target audience #1 and realize quickly that these aren't "your people" then okay. You

TARGETED APPROACH

Targeted Approach

Inner Circle (people who already know, like and trust you)

Warm Leads (past clients, etc.)

Target Market #1

Target Market #2

Target Market #3

Name: ______________________ Date: ______________

wealthyspeakerschool.com

regroup, and move on to target audience #2 and then #3. You are not married to any one idea. You test, have success or failure, and then adjust.

Note: When I say test I mean real test. Not "I sent out one e-mail to ten different companies in that industry and they didn't bite." That's like planting one row of seeds in a field. A true test is that you work a market for several months, perhaps sending multiple e-mails, a whole field full of seeds. We'll talk more about that in Chapter 12, Selling Yourself.

11

Developing a Successful Funnel

Building a Database

Everything you do in this business needs to have a strategy behind it. Here is a great question to post on your bulletin board: "Is this task getting me to where I want to go?" Many people spend time on the low pay-off activities and forget to do some of the most integral things that can help grow their business, like building a database.

Your Customer Relationship Manager (CRM)

From day one of your business, you should be adding names to a database and putting them into categories or "tags." Are they "speaking prospects," "book prospects," "friends," etc.? You may want to categorize your paying clients by year (20XX Keynote Client) so it's easy to pull them all up at the end of the year to recap or to send holiday greetings. If you aren't putting names and e-mails into a database, you are going to miss opportunities down the road.

If you aren't putting names and e-mails into a database, you are going to miss opportunities down the road.

Over the years here at The Wealthy Speaker School we have struggled to find "the one," that CRM we feel comfortable recommending to emerging speakers. For more advanced speakers, there is Active Campaign; that's what we use and really love it. But I have to admit, I haven't tapped its fullest capabilities (yet)!

Clients and students use Pipedrive, Hubspot, Zoho, but there are so many good ones to choose from. The key is to use whatever CRM you choose – on a daily basis. Why, because a CRM is only as good as its user.

A CRM is only as good as its user.

When you research CRMs, make sure that you know what criteria you will want. For instance, do you want a CRM that will send out a sequence of e-mails once an audience member signs up for something? You'll want to make sure it can do that. Do you want to ensure that you can build "template" e-mails and documents in order to merge all of the details when putting together a speaking agreement. Can you customize the fields? Can you "tag" clients and then search the tags. Those are some basics. When you see all that a CRM can do for you in terms of managing "deals" and showing you how much business is in your pipeline, you'll want to be realistic with yourself about what features you will actually use. If you get a CRM that is too advanced for you, it might feel overwhelming and you may not want to use it.

Your first stop once you have your CRM (some of you might use a spreadsheet until you have one) is gathering information from your prospects into customized fields. Here are some of the fields that you might want customized in your CRM and don't forget to check out Frankie's 14 in Chapter 12 to see which of his suggestions might work for you.

- Organization (this and all of the standard info like address, etc., is already set up)
- Contact Name (if there are multiple meeting planners, you can easily set up a group)
- Date of Next Meeting (make sure that you put it in a format that you can easily search)
- Location of Next Meeting (what city)

- Planning Month (when will they be doing their planning – use a drop-down list for this so you can easily search everyone planning in July)
- Number of Speakers (they use at their event)
- Fee Quoted (hopefully you are quoting straight off your fee schedule)
- Industry Type (you may want to set this up as a drop-down list for easy searching)

When your conversation with the client leads to a speaking agreement, you'll have most of the data already in set fields so that you just merge the information into an agreement template.

If you intend to sell books or an online course, you'll need to ensure that your CRM works with your shopping cart software that you build into your website.

Before buying anything, think through your needs and your long-term goals. Knowing these factors will help you choose the software that is most effective for you. Whatever software you choose, make sure that the contacts can be downloaded into other applications, should you change your mind later on.

Building Your List

There are many ways to go about getting more people into your CRM. It's important to be clear about the purpose of your list when setting it up. Are these people going to book you for speeches? Are they going to buy products from you later on? If you intend to write a book that everyone would benefit from, then you'll want everyone from your audiences to be added to your list.

Imagine this scenario.

Bo Simpkins attends your presentation at his corporate conference. He likes what you have to say and scans the QR code you have embedded into your PowerPoint so he can get your freebie/giveaway/lead magnet (see below).

Bo receives an e-mail immediately with the giveaway. (*Note:* This is where most speakers stop the process.)

You tag Bo in your CRM as "audience member" and you send a series of e-mails. Some are designed for him to get to know you better (indoctrination), and some are leading to the purchase of your book (a pretty light sell). But if Bo doesn't purchase your book, he still gets your weekly e-mail with tips about your topic. He knows he can unsubscribe at any time using the button at the bottom of each tip you send out.

Two years later Bo is in a different position with the company and is still getting your tips. He recommends you for another speaking engagement. Sweet!

All of this happened because your CRM worked and because you have been nurturing this relationship now for a couple of years. How many more Bos might be out in your audiences?

In order to build your list, your database, your CRM, take advantage of every speech using the following techniques.

- The "Help Me" Speech
- Feedback Forms/postcards (low tech)
- Text to service or QR Code scanner (lead magnet)

The "Help Me" Speech: Ask for the Business

Thom Winninger, who was a master at getting spin-off gigs from each engagement, taught me something *huge* many, many years ago. I call it the "help me" speech and have tweaked it some, but many speakers have used Thom's technique effectively to build their businesses. Sadly, Thom passed away in 2021, but his impact will live on.

When you are nearing the end of your presentation, preferably right before your closing story, insert the "help me" statement, or something like it, to let the audience know that you do this for a living and you'd love their help. Here's the "help me" line.

> As you can see I am passionate about ______________ (your topic). If you know of any company or association who could benefit

from this material, please come and hand me your business card afterwards.

That's it. Two lines that if missed could cost you thousands in spin-off business from every single event. Be strategic about every event. Ask, "How can I turn this into more business?"

Be strategic about every event. Ask, "How can I turn this into more business?"

People want to help you and they also want a reason to come up and talk to you afterwards. You need to plant seeds. You need to tell them how they can help you. So you are just allowing them to do what is natural and you are being specific about what they can do for you. First rule of business is "ask for the sale." When people hand you their cards, write down the details of what they say on the back (April event, 500 CEOs) so that you don't forget when you are following up. And one more thing ... *Follow up!*

A Note about the "help me" speech: You may feel that the "help me" speech is not a great idea for some corporate audiences. The meeting planner hired you to do a job and although it's only two lines, it's inappropriate. I would suggest that you be more vigilant about doing the help me speech in the beginning of your career and, most especially, when you are doing free speeches. Later in your career, it may no longer be necessary or appropriate.

In the next Chapter, you'll read about Betska K-Burr, the leadership expert, and how she ran her own showcase. She was the first speaker I ever represented. Betska was a really smart business woman who had come out of an executive position at 3M. She taught me a lot about business. The one thing that helped us grow so quickly was that she was great at asking for business from the platform. When I started working for her, she handed me a huge stack of business cards. They were all warm leads that she had collected giving her "help me" speech that she had learned from Thom Winninger. I spent my first three months working with Betska following up those warm leads and they filled our pipeline for the next three years.

I have an extremely high-tech gathering device for collecting those business cards – the one and only plastic Ziploc baggie, usually snack size.

I put a label on it – name of event and date – before going to the event and come back with a baggie full of leads. After I have followed up, scanned them, and added them to my Active Campaign database, they go back into the baggie, in case I ever need to track down a business card. A business card scanner can speed up the process if you are getting a lot of cards – and many CRMs have an app so you can scan the card right from your phone.

Feedback Forms – Postcards

This is a tip for speakers in the early stages of their business and you may decide not to use this once you have a solid lead magnet in place.

Getting the entire audience list could be beneficial. Using a feedback form guarantees most of the audience will respond and you'll get information beyond a database entry. There are five uses for feedback forms:

1. To find out what the audience likes and doesn't like about your presentation,
2. To gather testimonials,
3. To gather names and contact information for your database,
4. To get referrals, and
5. To get more business with this audience.

1. **Audience Feedback** – Asking your audience what they liked and what can be improved about your speech is very helpful, especially in the beginning of your career. Resist the urge to concentrate on the 1% of negative feedback when you have 99% positive. But always ask yourself if the information could be useful to you. You will rarely please 100% of the people in your audience, so don't be too concerned about every piece of negative feedback. Always be willing to learn and grow. And please note, every speaker bombs every once in a while. Know that you are not alone.

Every speaker bombs every once in a while. Know that you are not alone.

2. **Testimonials** – When asking for testimonials, ask the question, "What will you do differently as a result of this presentation?"

or "What have you learned that you will apply?" You want testimonials rich with ROI not a bunch saying "You are a good speaker." Every speaker has those. (You might also ask for permission to use the testimonial.)

3. **Database Building** – When asking for contact information, be sure to gather the minimum data - name and e-mail. If you can get their position in the company, and a phone number, that's helpful too.

4. **Referrals** – Although you do your "help me" speech, you can also ask for referrals on your feedback form. The standard line, "Who do you know who could benefit from xyz?" would work.

5. **More Business with this Audience** – You could also ask the group what else you might do for them and list the topics that you could come back to deliver at a later date.

Try your feedback form a few times and then tweak it. If you find you're not getting enough back, you might be asking for too much. These forms might be better suited for a longer session. A short keynote may not be as appropriate for a feedback form, you may want to opt for a lead magnet and/or some sort of "leave behind" instead.

"Text To" Service or QR Code – Lead Magnet

There are a lot of ways for you to capture your audiences' names and e-mail addresses. First, you want to make sure that you have a captivating lead magnet for them to sign up for. What do you have that they might want? Maybe it's a Tip Sheet - "Top 10 Ways to Lower Your Stress" - maybe it's a quiz or an audit - "What's Your Confidence Index? Take the quiz." Wouldn't you want to know? Your goal with your lead magnet is to offer something irresistible and to work it into your presentation and "sell" it. *Note:* During a keynote, try to have just one call to action. In a full-day session you could offer your lead magnet more than once, and do a feedback form but that may be too much for a 45-90-minute session. Our school's website specialist, Lauren Pibworth, and I did a podcast called "Creating Lead Magnets that Get Results" for a deeper dive on this topic - check the Bonus PDF for the link.

A "Text To" service allows people to "text jane to 2186" and receive a download of some kind. During this process the service will grab the name and e-mail. But I think a QR code might be less finicky and may work more seamlessly in different countries. But note, by the time the ink is dry on this book, there will be a new and better way, I'm sure.

A QR scan code is something you can place up on the screen during your presentation and have the audience pick up their phones, open their camera, scan the code, and follow the instructions from there (which asks for their name and e-mail).

You can also use a QR code to have people connect with you directly on LinkedIn (grab your QR code right from your LinkedIn phone app). You'll still want to get their e-mail via LinkedIn by offering an irresistible freebie. This just adds one more step, but connecting on LinkedIn might be a part of your strategy. If you do this, be sure to check out the profiles of the people who have connected with you and start a meaningful dialogue with them.

You'll test out various options and decide which service suits you and your style best.

And if you are technology adverse, you might circle back to the old-school feedback form idea. But these may not be ideal for a large keynote. Always ask the meeting organizer if they are doing a feedback form, and you may opt for something else if they have their own.

The meeting coordinator can often be your ally when it comes to promoting something to your audience. They may want the audience to purchase your books (keeping your message live), and, therefore, will direct people to your book signing table or "autograph" session. Perhaps they purchase books for everyone up front (see Chapter 14 for more on that). They typically want people to engage with your material, so these freebies can be supported by your key contact.

SHAWN CASEMORE

Finding/Closing Spin-off Business

I started speaking professionally in 2009. Admittedly in those early days I was a bit naïve. A successful speaking engagement to me meant that at the end of a talk, the meeting planner was happy, attendees seemed excited, and the check cleared the bank.

Once the friendly smiles were gone and the check was deposited, however, aside from a few spin-offs, I was often left to start the slow climb to finding my next engagement.

I was doing the traditional things – outreach to new associations to suggest speaking at their event, nurturing existing leads, connecting with past clients to share new ideas and talks.

Although these were and are still effective strategies for generating new opportunities, they result in hills and valleys of business. I knew there had to be an easier way to generate spin-off business, whether it was more speaking or consulting, so I tested several strategies to try to engage with more attendees.

What I learned was that by making three simple changes in my presentation, I could generate more spin-off business than I knew what to do with.

Here are the three steps that had the greatest impact.

1. Once the host read my bio, I thanked the person introducing me, mentioned my name again, and shared my brief value proposition. For example: "Thanks for that, Susan. Hello everyone, my name is Shawn Casemore, and I help business owners and sales leaders accelerate their sales results." Then I would move into my opening story.
2. At the end of every event, I mentioned a simple takeaway that would act as a resource for participants to execute what they'd heard me discuss. For example: "If you're interested in a copy of my twelve steps to sales success, send me an e-mail or a message on LinkedIn right now, and I'll send it over tomorrow."

3. Following the event, once returning to my home office, I began reaching out to anyone I had connected with at the event. If the person I reached out to was in a position to hire me, I would suggest we speak as there was something I didn't share in my talk that I thought they'd find helpful.

Through these three simple steps, I increased my revenue by 30% the following year with additional speaking engagements and consulting work.

Sometimes it's the simplest things that get us the most return. And don't forget the tips from Chapter 14 on how to leverage every event.

Consistency with All Marketing Is Key

All of the ideas in this book are useful, but only if you follow through on them with some consistency. Discipline is hard for many of us, but I've learned that without it, your office can fall apart very quickly. You may be losing business simply because you are not taking action in a consistent manner. When things start slipping through the cracks, eventually it leads to client's not being serviced properly, deals lost, or something worse that makes you miss an engagement.

Decide which of these techniques you will use to build your database and then do it consistently. And make sure that your "back end" is set up for follow up. If you fill your database full of prospects but then send them nothing, how is that helpful?

Don't let business fall through the cracks because you are not doing things in a consistent manner.

When you have business cards that you gathered from a speaking event, that is low hanging fruit and should be followed up immediately! In fact, send them an e-mail from the plane.

12

Selling Yourself

Launching your speaking business, once you've done the work to get Ready and Aim at what you want, is akin to selling – yourself. Promoting oneself is not easy for most people, so try to think of yourself as the spokesperson for a great product, a product you believe in – you. In this Chapter we'll explore some ideas to get you, your name, and your value out in front of the people you want to help.

Checking Your Mindset Before the Sale

We discussed the Wealthy Speaker's mindset in good detail back in Chapter 2, but it is worth repeating in terms of your sales mindset. And on that note, before we dive too deeply into mindset, here's a coach's question to get you started and get you thinking about sales.

What do you think about sales?

Some people don't even realize that they have this icky "ewww, I can't *sell* someone" mentality which means that they are putting themselves in a difficult position. Because guess what? In order to get on stages, a sale needs to be made.

But I don't think you have to call it "selling." You can think of it like matchmaking what you offer with what they need. Do we have a match?

Remember from earlier, your thoughts equal your results. So, if you change your thoughts you can change your results.

Use your Thought Model Worksheet to ensure you are approaching your market with the right thought.

What's Your Selling Superpower?

Not everybody is great on the phone. Not everyone is good at working a room at a live networking event. What is your selling superpower?

Let's give you some options.

1. E-mail marketing. Some of my clients, like Judi Holler, are very good at e-mail.
2. Phone. Smiling and dialing. My client, Ryan Estis, was an amazing salesperson therefore smiling and dialing came easy to him. If you have a fear of rejection, this may not be your superpower.
3. Networking. If you can walk into a meeting room with 100 people, make meaningful connections and walk away with prospective business, then networking may be your superpower. My client, Amanda Hammett, would come back with two or three solid leads from every event she went to.
4. Social media. Many speakers today are seeing business come in from Instagram, Facebook, LinkedIn, TikTok and YouTube. If this is working for you, then double down and make it a part of your ongoing strategy.

When you find something that you are good at – you must double down and do it more frequently.

There are definitely other possibilities here, so don't limit yourself to these four superpowers.

But what's the key? When you find something that you are good at – you must double down and do it more frequently.

Let's say networking is your superpower. Then you commit to attending networking events that can put you in front of buyers two to four times per month. These go on your calendar and you keep that commitment. That is how you start to build momentum, with consistent action.

If your superpower is e-mail, then commit to sending a certain number of e-mails each week. One thing we do quite well in our School is hold people accountable to their goals. If you want to be speaking x times per year, then reaching out to x people per week is required. This is all math.

Your Approach

Bringing Value to an Organization

When you are first starting out in the industry you will most likely be thinking about booking one speech at a time. You're really finding your way in the industry and you have to start somewhere. However, if you can take a broader approach from the beginning and think about the question, "How can I bring *value* to this organization?" then you'll be on the right track, and thinking bigger. Although the techniques outlined are designed to book "a speech," always be thinking of the big picture with a company.

JANE ATKINSON

Selling Beyond the Speech

In the early days of your speaking business you'll definitely focus on booking a speech, delivering a speech, and getting your systems down. But, once you have the basics, you may decide to sell beyond the speech. What might that look like? Well, perhaps you are offering packages instead of speeches?

A package may include:

- 45-minute keynote,
- A deep dive webinar discussion of the content,
- Xx Copies of your books (if you have one),

- Worksheets that you customize, or
- One-on-one coaching or consulting to further enhance the learning.

And when you're feeling ready to add more consider:

- A series of customized video messages,
- Access to your club or membership program,
- Leadership retreats, or
- Train the trainer.

As your repertoire of products and services grows, so will your package offerings grow. Laurie Guest and I have done podcasts about Sweet Spot Pricing that allow you to build out three options for the client. Perhaps option #1 is simply the speech? Whatever they have requested. And then you have two more options that are packages, with the third option being everything but the kitchen sink.

Laurie's advice has you selling the middle package – that's the sweet spot. So you might price Option 3 quite high to make Option 2 look perfect. Check out Laurie Guest's podcast on Sweet Spot Pricing for more – you'll find that in the Bonus materials.

You'll want to name your packages based on outcomes. Let's say you are being asked to speak on communication. Option 1 might be: Communication Keynote. Option 2 might be: Enhanced Communication Breakthrough. Option 3 might be: Communication Breakthrough Plus.

The bottom line is that your work can go so much further than simply speeches. If you want to expand your learning once you have mastered the basics, be sure to check out my book, *Scaling Your Speaking Business: 10 Strategies for Earning More While Doing Less.*

Matching Versus Cold Calling

As discussed earlier, a great mindset technique is to think about sales differently. When you are preparing to make your phone calls or send query e-mails you want to be wearing your attraction hat rather than your sales hat. It wouldn't hurt for you to know how to sell, but, basically, what if you were calling the prospect to see whether or not the client has a need that your services match?

Does that take the pressure off?

Get yourself into attraction or matching mode by thinking about the value that you have to offer (you are the expert) before picking up the phone. Have Worksheet 17, The Value You Offer handy and it will help keep you focused when making calls. Now that you are in the right mode, you're ready to start making calls.

Some of my clients can suffer from the "who do I think I am" imposter syndrome when approaching a money conversation with a client. Let's make sure that it's clear to you (and your brain) exactly why they should pay you in this next exercise.

THE VALUE YOU OFFER

List the value that you bring to an organization. Organize your list and print it out in bullet form and post it in front of you before picking up the phone to make "matching" calls. Remember when you are talking to prospective clients give them stories that they can relate to and relay to others.

The Value I Offer: Sample

1. I provide a strategy for increasing sales.
2. My strategy covers three areas that are integral to selling success: authenticity, integrity, and value.
3. My average client's ROI is a 25% increase in customer loyalty.
4. My client, ABC company, used these techniques to close two $50,000 deals within a one-week period.
5. I've written several books on this topic.
6. I have xxx experience and background.

The Value I Offer

1. ______________________________

____

____

2. ______________________________

____

____

3. ______________________________

____

____

Call-Send-Call – Still Works!

When I first started in the business, over thirty years ago, the call-send-call method was the primary way of getting booked into speeches. As I said, I learned this technique from Thom Winninger, the person whose recipe I followed diligently.

Back then, you'd call someone to establish a need, send materials via mail or courier, and then call back. It was effective! I think for the most part it will always work, but the way the client makes the decision will continue to become more sophisticated. They rely on referrals, seeing a speaker in person, and word of mouth predominantly. Your goal is to have your outreach (and social media) be so consistent that when they come to needing your topic, you are top of mind.

There is a basic seven-step process that outlines the call-send-call method.

1. Identify the prospect.
2. Call or e-mail them and find out when they are planning for their next event.
3. Establish yourself as an expert on a topic that may be of interest to that group.
4. Confirm that they can afford you.

5. When they are in the planning stages, provide them with links to your website and speech options. Ask them what they need to see to make their decision. They may require that you show them some video.
6. Find out when the decision will be finalized.
7. Follow up at the appropriate time.

If there is some lag time during this process, you might send them a current article or podcast that you did to keep your name top of mind. Try to remind them about your expertise without stalking them.

But before you ever pick up the phone, send an e-mail, or connect on LinkedIn, you want to get clear on your value (Worksheet 17) and make sure that you have the right approach. You also want to research as much as you can about their event. If the information is readily available on their website, don't waste their time asking the (where and when is your next meeting) questions. That's annoying.

Who to Call: Why Start with Associations?

Remember the work we did back in Ready: Chapter 5, Positioning? Well, that is going to come into play now. If you narrow down your "people" to teachers and nurses, then you have a place to start. It's so helpful to be focused when beginning your outreach.

The best way to get in front of teachers and nurses is through the associations that support and oversee them. And that is why we start with associations.

Let's say you deliver an epic presentation for 250 nurses at a state or provincial nursing convention. Could that not also lead to work at dozens of hospitals? I think so, and that is why we typically recommend you start your outreach campaigns with associations.

Here are a few more benefits of working the associations.

- They are consistent – almost every association has at least one meeting or convention each year.

- It's easy to find out from their websites when the meetings are held and if they use outside speakers. This is where knowing your competition will come in handy.
- Many associations frequently hire professional speakers.
- Association audiences are full of hundreds or thousands of people from corporations. Why not speak to people from 500 different companies? The exposure couldn't be any better.

You can Google for most any associations you are looking for. Or if you want the work to be done for you, check out Sam Richter's search tool called "IntelNgin" using the link we provide for you in the Bonus materials.

Being able to find out more information on the association or company you'd like to engage with is extremely helpful.

You can also buy directories of associations for about $250-$500. You might consider paying a little more to get your updates electronically, so that your list is as current as possible. Be sure to ask around before investing.

When times get tough, no matter what the circumstance, if you focus on providing value, you will survive and thrive.

Remember that associations need your help, they need the value you are bringing to the table. When times get tough, no matter what the circumstance, if you focus on providing value, you will survive and thrive. When disruptions occur, associations get hit hard and if you can bring them something that will help them keep members or attract new ones, you will be very useful to them!

How Else Can You Get Their Attention?

Let's imagine that your prospective clients - association meeting planners - are getting an average of 100 e-mails per day. That's probably not too far from the truth. Now imagine how many meetings they have to attend and how many voice messages from speakers and speakers' bureaus they would receive once they return. You can see that getting their attention is going to be a challenge, so you need to think outside of the box. Use the list of attention getters below to start your creative juices flowing.

- Call and leave an after-hours message – short, sweet, and to the point. "This is Jo Smith calling. I'm the author of *Selling with Integrity* and I'm calling about your July 20XX conference. If this topic is of interest, please check out my website at *JoSmith.com* and drop me a line or call (555) 555-1999."
- Offer them something for free. Jo Smith might have an article that the association would like to post on its LinkedIn page.
- Send them a postcard.
- Send them a one- to two-line e-mail that asks one question, such as "Is sales a topic of interest for the July 20XX event?" It gives them an option to reply very quickly.
- Connect with them on LinkedIn.
- Send them a bulky package (candy or something) with a postcard or letter with a link to your video. (Here's a little popcorn while you watch.)
- Try to meet them in person. Attend one of their events or offer your services to their office.
- Send them a voice or video message via social media.

Word of mouth is one of the most powerful marketing methods.

- Invite them to one of your speaking engagements.
- If you know a speaker who has already spoken to the group, ask them to put in a good word for you. Word of mouth is one of the most powerful marketing methods.
- Partner with a sponsor who wants to get in front of the same groups you do. Maybe there is a sales CRM software that aligns perfectly with Jo's message.
- Comment on things that they care about in their social media feeds. Without being a stalker but just enough for them to think, "I keep seeing this Jo Smith. Who is that?"

Cold Calling – Making It Work

If phone selling is your superpower, then let's get making those calls. How many calls are you committing to each week? When you decide, place some time on your calendar for outreach and then commit to keeping your promise to yourself.

Once you have someone on the phone, be sure to make notes about the person in your CRM so you can continue the relationship every time you talk. Remember that this call is about meeting *their* needs. Don't "pitch slap" them (thank you Jennifer Darling for that term). This means don't call them and start spouting all of the great things about yourself. The goal is to begin building the relationship and that won't fly well if you start off with a pitch.

Your opening might be something like, "This is Jo Smith calling about your July 20XX event. Do you have a minute?" Once they give you the go ahead, then ask questions to establish a need. If they say "No, this isn't a good time," do your best to reschedule. You will often find that they are not the key contact. Some key questions are listed below, and, please, you must be respectful of people's time. You might only get one or two questions answered when you notice that they are anxious to hang up.

- Are you the person who is in charge of booking the speakers for your upcoming conferences? If not, who?
- When is your next event? (Hopefully you already know this.)
- When will you be planning for this event? If they say six months from now, try to gain more information about the event and schedule a time to call back.
- How many paid speakers will you book for this event? "Paid" is the key word. If this association doesn't pay its speakers, then move on.
- How is the decision made? By one person? Who? By committee?
- What topics will you want to include in this year's conference? Ask if your topic would be of interest to this audience. Make sure you state the benefits of the speech.

- What is your budget for each speaker? Breakout? Keynote? Ask about your specific slot.
- In what city will the event be held? You should know this ahead of time.
- How many people will attend?
- What is the demographic? What job(s) do they do?
- What is your theme? This is your opportunity to talk about how your speech would fit. Keep asking questions about the group's needs to keep your contact's interest. You may even suggest they go to your website while on the line with you.
- Who did you have speak last year? Try to know this ahead of time as well and be prepared to discuss how you might follow up with that speaker.
- When will you make the decision regarding speakers?
- May I send you a link? To website, video, etc.
- When will you be reviewing my materials?
- When should I get back in touch? How? Phone, e-mail?

The Click – The Good Kind

Hopefully the prospect doesn't hang up on you – that would be the undesirable click. The good kind of click is when you are talking to a prospect and you feel a shift in energy when they become interested – as opposed to being polite. That is when you know you have their interest and can start building a relationship. If you never get the "click," then it's an uphill battle.

Do your research. Bring up specific details about the company, or things that you've learned about them personally from their LinkedIn profile. You also need to listen carefully and respond to the needs they express. Don't forget to mention your value/benefits, but phrase it in terms of their needs. Make it about them. For instance, you might say, "Joanne, when I was studying your association's website, I noticed that you had a lot of sales training scheduled throughout the year for your people. Would a program that could help them build 25% more customer loyalty be helpful to your audience?"

The Other End of the Line

Picture the client hanging up from your conversation and picking up the phone five minutes later to have the same conversation with another speaker or bureau. You must always be aware that they may be overwhelmed by calls from people. Meeting planners are looking for any reason to put you in the "yes" or "no" pile just so that they can clear their desk or to-do list.

Meeting planners are looking for any reason to put you in the "yes" or "no" pile just so that they can clear their desk or to-do list.

If they are not really interested, they may use the "Can you send me something?" line to get you off the phone. If that happens, try to qualify a little more before hanging up. You need to be sympathetic to what they go through in a day. Show them that you get it. "Those damn speakers just won't stop calling ☺." The more you can understand their position, the better you will be able to build the relationship. Remember to place notes about the conversation in your database for future reference.

A few years back, Mark Levin, Executive Vice President of Chain Link Fence Manufacturers Institute, described planning for his institute's annual meeting.

> When our association's annual meeting is coming up, we start getting intense about six months out. That's when we have to start making final decisions on programs, speakers, off-property functions, etc. Although we (as a small association) try to book speakers that are geographically close to our meeting site, it's certainly not the determining factor. In recent years we've been getting many speakers who quote us airfare-inclusive fees that make it easier to make a final decision.
>
> In general, our "outside" (outside of our specific industry) speakers are booked based on three or four key issues.
>
> 1. The right topic for our group (usually humor or personal development).

2. The right delivery, based on one or more criteria (in order of priority):
   - I've seen them live,
   - I've seen their website (and the video of them speaking),
   - Someone I trust *completely* has seen and recommended them, or
   - I check out their YouTube channel if they have one and their social footprint.
3. The right price. (I consider who might sponsor their session.)
4. How the first phone call felt? (Were they interested, responsive, and friendly; did they ask me the right questions about our group?)

The Simple Things Get You in the Door

Surprisingly enough, back when I was selling speakers, I started many conversations with the weather. Living in a place like Canada is an advantage because your U.S. clients are curious and can't help but ask you some questions. The key is to allow the relationship to grow gradually. Know the needs of your client well before you start providing solutions. If you present yourself like the answer to all of their problems – before you even know their problems – then you are going to lack credibility with them.

When I was selling speakers, my goal was always to build the relationship first and to pitch my speaker second. The best-case scenario is that you have a friendship happening before they even look at your materials. You want them to give you an honest answer about whether or not you are a contender.

Know the needs of your client well before you start providing solutions.

FRANK SOMMA

Frankie's 14 CRM Tips

People do business with people they like. So how does one become more likable? It's never about what you say. It's about how folks feel after an encounter with you. So how do we help people to feel more in tune with us after each encounter? We ask questions about their favorite subjects, themselves, their families, their interests, and their passions.

Back when I was a little baby salesperson, I discovered ACT! It was one of the first CRMs (Customer Relationship Managers) to hit the market. I bought it, went to the NYC public library with my hair slicked back, my wide-shouldered double-breasted suit, 20lb "portable" computer and my new program on those 5 ¼ inch floppy disks, and learned it.

While CRMs are essential for tracking appointments, follow-ups, notes, and to-do lists, they are also built for cataloging conversations, proposals, e-mails, and multiple contacts in an account. Apart from or integrated with your ERP (Enterprise Resource Planning), they also hold the essentials like addresses and suite numbers, extensions, mobile numbers, e-mail addresses, titles, and so on.

What gave me chills on that fateful day in the library was the customization ACT! offered me. I was able to create fields to hold customized information and Frankie's Fabulous Fourteen was born. My fabulous fourteen is a list of fourteen items I wanted to learn about my client. Non-business things like what school they attended and do they have kids or pets. I wanted to know their favorite sports team, vacation spot, or opera.

This was a game-changer. No longer did I call my largest accounts with the same old diatribe. "Hi Debbie, just checking in to see that we are taking good care of you. Is everything okay with our services?"

"Yes Frank, all good. Thanks for calling." What did that do to ingratiate me, my company, or my services to Debbie? Not much.

Instead, with my CRM open to my custom fields, I gently asked questions during each call and recorded pertinent answers. After a little time, I was able to quickly review my Fab-14 in my CRM before calling and my calls to Debbie went like this: "Hi Deb, how are things?"

"Good, Frank, thanks."

"Excellent, Debbie. By the way, I just read an article in *The Times* that said that nursing is one of the top five growth areas for the next ten years. That's great news for Joseph, right? Isn't he just about finished with nursing school?"

"Yes, that is great for him. He is graduating this spring but thinking about going for his masters."

"Wow, you must be very proud."

And with that, the conversation goes on with Debbie talking about her son and the specialties he is interested in and where he is thinking about working, etc.

What did *that* conversation do to ingratiate me, my company, and my service to Debbie? A LOT!

Let me offer one caveat. I *am* sincerely interested in Debbie's son's progress. I love hearing the pride in her voice as she tells me about him. I feel that way with all my clients and their sports stories, pet anecdotes, and family vacations. I love people and want to hear more. Kinky Friedman, one of my favorite wise-cracking authors said, "You can't fake sincerity." That's the key here. Your sincerity comes through and even though your clients are talking about themselves, because you prompted them and exhibited sincere interest, they will like *you* more.

Here is Frankie's Fabulous Fourteen. Feel free to use some, add some, or replace some but whatever you do, implement some form of this into your CRM and watch the relationships and your business bloom.

Frankie's Fabulous Fourteen

(Add these customized fields to your favorite CRM)

1. Hometown
2. # 1 Hobby
3. Marital status, spouse's name
4. Kids or Grandkids (as many names as possible)
5. Birthday
6. Associations or clubs
7. Favorite Charity
8. Movie, Television or Music interests
9. Vacation; when and where

10. What car do they drive
11. Favorite sports team or figure
12. Current Residence, City, State
13. College
14. Pets

Follow Up Is King

You likely know that follow up is king. Without follow up, you are going to be seed planting forever and there will be no harvest. When you are following up with a client, you don't have to be a stalker but you don't want it to be a "one and done" e-mail.

If you have left several voice messages and not received a call back, try a quick query e-mail.

> John, I've left a couple of messages – don't want you to think I'm a pest. No doubt you are super busy. Are you thinking about your XYZ event?

When you are following up with a client, don't be a stalker.

That's it. Not two or three lines about how great you are, just a question that they can hit reply and say, "Sorry, Jane, I haven't had a chance. Touch base with me next week."

Jen McDonough, who runs The Wealthy Speaker School, and whose story you heard in Chapter 2, uses this cadence when following up e-mails.

1. E-mail 1: goes out
2. Wait 7 days: E-mail 2
3. Wait 14 days: E-mail 3

You may very well follow the idea that it takes fourteen touches before a prospect buys and we do have students who are sending many more than three e-mails. This is just one idea to get you started.

Consider other options aside from e-mail if you haven't gotten anything back. Perhaps you connect via LinkedIn, leave a voice-mail, send a postcard – see list of options earlier in this Chapter.

In his Masters Class for our school, my friend David Avrin said that it's often e-mail number two or three that seems to get noticed. So, bottom line, please do not give up after one e-mail.

Never assume that you know what's going on at the client's end. In fact, assume that you don't have a clue. They might be busy with another project, or a personal matter, but when you have a warm lead on the line go cold, don't let the thought "they don't want me" allow you to shut down your follow up. Keep the lines of communication open, keep trying!

JANE ATKINSON

Top 12 Marketing Strategies

As I've said before there is no better form of marketing than a great speech. Getting two to three spin-offs from each engagement is your goal and your marketing becomes much easier. Until the spin-off train is rolling ahead, here is a list of a dozen top strategies to keep you in your clients' thoughts.

1. Sales Calls or E-mail Queries – We've outlined these for you previously in this Chapter.
2. The Article Placement Strategy – Place articles in your target industry's publications, newsletters, or blogs.
3. Direct Mail – Series of postcards or articles. Maybe you have a hot fifty list of prospects to send your book to?
4. Social Media – Pull people into your network with daily posts, lead magnets, and updates that establish you as the expert.
5. Shake the Trees – Work your inner circle and past clients to drum up new business. You should be talking to past clients a minimum of twice a year to stay in touch (even if it's just a Valentine's card).
6. Outbound Broadcasts – Send out e-Tips or videos to your database that help drive people to your website and often they will result in business.
7. Quiz or Audit – Follow up your lead magnets with a personal e-mail to score a discovery call.

8. Media Darling – Be quoted as an expert and be seen by the media as someone who can comment on your area of expertise. (More on PR in Chapter 13.)
9. Freebie Speeches – The Rubber Chicken Circuit. Speak to anyone who will listen to generate momentum.
10. Marketing Calendar – Develop a twelve-month system to ensure that you are "touching" clients on a regular basis.
11. Podcast – A brilliant way to bring new subscribers to your door on a regular basis.
12. Showcases or Webinars – Run your own public events to generate cash flow and gain access to companies. (See Flashpoint Betska K-Burr, below, for more on this).

BETSKA K-BURR

Running Your Own Showcase

When I was working as a Business Manager for Betska K-Burr, my very first speaker, we decided to put together a showcase in our hometown of London, Ontario, to help her gain more awareness as a leadership and recognition expert. We had made some inroads in our own backyard because of her speaking on the rubber chicken circuit, but we really needed to build momentum.

I asked the local radio station with our demographic to get involved. We offered them free admission for their staff and gave them a number of tickets to hand out to their clients (mostly small business owners). In turn they gave us some free radio spots. We charged a small amount to attend and, as soon as the radio announcements kicked in, registrations started rolling in.

We also partnered with our local business magazine and had them advertise for us (quarter page ad) in lieu of a sponsorship package that included some free seats for their staff and clients (also local business owners). They gave away a trial subscription at the event. All of our partners had their materials on hand and were allowed to put up banners and speak for three minutes each, before the headliner,

Betska. She would deliver her presentation about how to "Create Champions" in their teams (also the title of her book).

We invited the press to come free of charge and our local clients and prospects were also given complimentary seats. We arranged a barter with the hotel and AV company – allowing their clients and staff to come for free.

So our out-of-pocket expenses were handouts, coffee, and tea. That was it. We filled a good-sized meeting room with about 150 people and everyone loved the event – and Betska. We closed several pieces of business later that week and got the momentum that we desired. I don't recall if it was a direct result of that event, but later that year Betska got the cover story in the local business magazine. Think about how you can run showcases for your clients or the press and get sponsors to help fill the room for you! Many of the same principles could apply – finding sponsors, trading advertising for tickets, etc. – for running your own public seminars.

And don't forget you could always run your own "showcase" using a webinar or virtual program. If you run free webinars once a quarter, you are bound to book some discovery calls with people who are interested in your work. Just make sure you fill those audiences with prospective buyers.

I remember talking to speaking legend Glenna Salsbury about how she got started in speaking by running her own showcase (live event) in Scottsdale. Similar to us, she put 200 people into a hotel room and 30 years later she could attribute a big chunk (like 80% of her business) back to that original talk. When you run your showcase, being impressive is essential and if you don't think you are ready, then wait.

The Outcome – Rejection

At some point a decision will be made – you will get the engagement or you won't. If the answer is "not this year," remember, don't take it personally. You simply were not a match this year.

When a decision-maker tells you that you are not a good fit for their meeting this year, politely ask whether or not you will be considered in the future and schedule a reminder for next year. Don't argue or try to change their mind. Huge turn off!

When I was working at the speakers' bureau, agents would often tell me about speakers getting angry on the phone when they were told they would not be getting the booking. They had no idea the kind of impression this behavior left on the bureau agent. That agent, and that bureau, would *never* book that speaker now. And decision-makers feel similarly.

And what might have led to the decision of them going a different direction? Perhaps it was your marketing (your website or video), maybe it didn't have enough focus for the topic they wanted. Or maybe your style didn't suit their needs. But what if you and your topic had absolutely nothing to do with it? What if the organizers decided that they needed someone who looked different than you, had a different skin color, gender, or background. These things are so far out of our control, we just have to let it go.

We can actually bring this conversation back into mindset and your thoughts about not getting a gig. Perhaps you react with "I'm not good enough" or maybe you make it mean something even more "I'll never have success in this business." Really examine your thoughts when you don't get an engagement. Why do this? Because when you move into conversations with the next prospect, you must be coming from a place of confidence and not rejection.

When you move into conversations with the next prospect, you must be coming from a place of confidence and not rejection.

When you are more intentional with your thought – "no problem, I'll get the next one" – and you move back into a feeling of confidence quickly, you will be in the best place possible to keep planting seeds and booking discovery calls.

13

Public Relations (PR)

Launch Your Message to the Masses

There are a number of ways to get your message out during the Launch phase. It all comes down to selling yourself – or at least your expertise. Securing press coverage sounds like an amazing idea, but will it put you in front of decision-makers, and, more importantly, will it book speeches?

Many people start their roll out with a book launch and that includes PR. If that's not the case for you, you might try some of the other "launch" techniques before tackling the press. Some speakers don't put a PR plan into place at all, and that's okay. Just skim this section for now and come back to it when needed. Or, pick out a few ideas and simply begin.

If you let the local media know that you are presenting a speech at the local insurance association, I doubt that will garner results. That doesn't answer the question "who cares?" But, if you've written a press release about how insurance companies are building trust with their clients during difficult times, well, maybe that's a hook.

Securing press coverage sounds like an amazing idea, but will it put you in front of decision-makers, and, more importantly, will it book speeches?

Building your expertise means getting in front of your target market and being seen as the expert. Maybe you can do that without the press. But, if you do land a slot on a national TV show talking about your expertise, you'll definitely want to use that photo or video on your website – instant clout!

With the polarized climate today, having several clips featuring you as a guest on Fox News or on CNN may be making an unintended statement about your political leanings. Just something to be aware of.

Writing a Column

I have a few clients and friends who write for big name journals and the consensus seems to be that the name recognition and "clout" from being a columnist does pay off. Perhaps not in "I read your last column and I want to book you" ways but more in credibility. My client, Stevie Ray, who is a National Columnist for *The Business Journals Newspapers,* says the results with his clients are more name recognition. "Oh, yeah. I've heard of him. I read his column."

Press Releases – The "So What?" Factor

The mistake that I see most speakers making is sending out a press release that does not answer the question "So what?" They don't tie it to anything relevant that the press can sink their teeth into. So you wrote a book? So you won an award? So you're speaking at a conference? So what? Give them a reason to have you on the show. Imagine the host saying, "It's mental health month and Frank King, the mental health comedian, is here to talk about how to lighten up even the most difficult conversations."

Have a very clear goal in mind when you start a press release and then work backwards thinking about how you can provide value to the press. They need a solid, steady stream of content for their readers or viewers and are always trying to find experts to weigh in on current events.

Expert Available for Comment

Journalists go to online services when they are seeking experts on particular topics. You might consider getting yourself listed with some of these services so that you can be found when they need you.

There's a service called HelpAReporter.com (HARO) that you can sign up for and receive notices from journalists who are seeking experts on particular topics. You'll have to dig through some e-mails, but it could really pay off.

Hiring an Agency or Publicist

Self-promotion is not easy for most people and it is a full-time job in and of itself. Hiring an agency or publicist can lighten your load. Some of the things you'll want to consider before hiring someone to help you promote yourself or your book are listed below.

- Do they know my market?
- Do they understand my goals?
- Do they have the contacts that I need?
- Do they have a good reputation?
- What is their track record?
- Can I "pay for performance?" Meaning you pay when they get results.
- Will they work hard for me or will I get lost in the pile?
- Who has used them with success? Try to find some of your own references as well as the ones they provide. Ask them for at least six people, then call the bottom of the list first.
- Will I have to sign a long-term contract? If so, then think very carefully. Many speakers have been completely dissatisfied with their PR firms, so make sure you have a trial period before locking into anything long term. Or better yet, use an agency on a project basis.

Not all PR agents are going to have wins every single time. Know your odds and exactly what activities your dollars are going towards. If the cost of your agency is so high that you have to mortgage your home, then don't do it. There are too many companies out there to choose from to take on more financial burden than you can handle. (You could always find a PR student.)

Always bring the costs of your PR agency back to something tangible. For example, I only have to book two speeches for this entire three-month campaign to pay for itself. If your goal is strictly to sell books, you may have to evaluate your costs closely.

There's no reason why you can't pick up the phone to call your local TV station and pitch them a "timely" idea.

There's just so much noise out there, competing for attention with the press. There's no reason why you can't pick up the phone to call your local TV station and pitch them a "timely" idea. And once there, ask some questions to discover how you can be a resource for them. I have many clients doing weekly television appearances or writing a monthly syndicated column and they say it has resulted in a small amount of speaking business.

14

You're Booked – Now What?

You've got a booking. That's great! Give yourself a pat on the back – and let's get back to work. Not only do you need to prepare for the engagement, so all is in place, you will still have work to do after you've received your standing ovation.

Flow of the Booking

Every time you book an engagement, a series of things should fall into place – either by doing them yourself or with help. As mentioned earlier, consistency is key so develop a system with a checklist and stick to it. And please note, as we've discussed, there is definitely a way to run your entire business electronically, so only develop paper files if it feels appropriate for you.

- **Agreement** – (See Agreements and Contracts later in this Chapter.) Agreements are a top priority because they bring in money and confirm that the client is serious. Agreements will always be the first and most important document you create. You may want to send a copy of your book (or other product) with every agreement to plant the seed about quantity discounts, so that they pre-purchase books for everyone. If you don't have a book to send, perhaps you go paperless on your agreements and have the client e-Sign?

If you have a paper file, leave a copy of the agreement in the file so that you can ensure that you follow through on what you have promised the client. If you have promised books or something extra as a part of the deal, then make a calendar note or task in your CRM to ship them two weeks prior to the event and put a reminder in the file.

- **Invoice** – You might send two invoices with your speaker's agreement. One is the deposit of 50% to hold your date and the second 50% is due on the day of the event. Copies go in your file.
- **Never rely on your memory** because eventually all of your engagements will run together, so you must have procedures in place to ensure that nothing falls through the cracks.
- **Client Folder** – If you aren't 100% electronic yet, prepare and label a client file folder. Keep your client files all one color so that they are easy to spot among other files. You might use a color that signifies wealth to you, like green or purple. Your label should have the client's name, the date and the city, so that five years from now – after several repeat engagements – you know which gig is which.
- **Leads Baggie/Envelope** – While you are making your label for the file, make a second one for the leads' baggie or envelope (where you will place business cards gathered at the event). If you prefer electronic leads gathering, take a photo of the business cards and hand them back. Or find people on social media (whatever platform you use most) right in the moment and connect.
- **Thank You Cards** – I know this is old school, but if you are making labels, you might as well make address labels for the client and the bureau and put them on your thank you card envelopes. It's a lovely gesture to hand write these from the road if you prefer. People don't get many handwritten letters any more. Don't forget to add the postage ahead of time so you can hand them over to the hotel staff or drop them in a mailbox before traveling to your next city.
- **Contact Management** – Make sure that you tag your client properly in your CRM, so that you can easily reference all clients for that year at once. Tag: 20XX Keynote Client or 20XX Training Client.

- **Event Details Form** – An Event Detail Form (paper) or page on your app or CRM (paperless) includes all of the information from the agreement: client details (cell numbers), event details (meeting room name, AV check time), travel details (flights, ground, hotel), and any other pertinent information or notes (e.g., UPS tracking for books shipped). You might keep it all in one place (see more on eSpeakers in Chapter 15) as that's what the eSpeakers Event CX app was designed for), or you might design your own system for this. What's important is that you use a system and keep a checklist of all things that need doing. eSpeakers does this for you, so there is really no need to reinvent the wheel.

BONUS DOWNLOAD

- **Expenses Envelope** – Unless you do a flat rate travel fee (recommended), keep an envelope inside your file for expenses. We don't love to nickel and dime clients, so avoid things like meals and incidentals. Just charge them for the larger items like air travel, ground transportation and hotel (typically charges are placed on their master account).
- **Handouts** – If you know at this point what handout you will use, then place the original in the paper file. Or, for paperless you can send the handout in a separate e-mail with the subject line: speech prep/handout/intro/photos, along with your bio, introduction, photo, and pre-program questionnaire if you have one. Making it easy for the client to find things on demand by using topic specific subject lines will be appreciated. Most of these items may be available on the meeting planners page on your website - if that's the case, send the link. Some speakers don't create the handout until closer to the program, that's okay too.
- **Introduction** – Keep a spare copy of your introduction in the paper file or be prepared to e-mail it to their phone or iPad. The MC will often forget to bring a copy to the meeting.
- **Product Ship Date** – Schedule a product ship date and make notes on what you plan to send.

That's a summary of what needs to go into your client file before you hit the road. You're getting everything set up as a system. Refer to your checklist at two weeks out, two days out and six hours before departure. No leaving it to the last minute in case there is something pertinent missing! Having a checklist that you refer to before departure will ensure you are not showing up frazzled for your speech.

Having a checklist that you refer to before departure will ensure you are not showing up frazzled for your speech.

Remember Neen James' story about running a speaking business from your phone (see Chapter 4)? This is entirely possible by moving all of these pieces onto the cloud and keeping files and records in the database rather than in a paper file. You decide what's perfect for you!

Leveraging Each Engagement

As you prepare for each audience you need to be thinking ahead – to the next booking, or your overall contact with this client. Is there more work to be done here? Perhaps some consulting?

Here are some ideas that can help increase your chances of more business spinning off from each presentation. These should also be a part of your speech prep process so that you are never missing opportunities.

- Once the client has chosen you for the presentation, ask them how long they want your message to stay with their audience? They should say "as long as possible" and this tees you up to talk about how you might develop a long-term program for this audience with some follow-up. Or perhaps they might pre-purchase books for everyone.
- Offer to meet with an inside group of people before your speech for a meal or a special workshop. This might include the Executive Group, Board of Directors, Inner Circle, etc.
- Request a meeting with the Big Cheese (President, CEO, Executive Director) and find out during that meeting how you can

customize your presentation to help them in their mission. This also adds to your credibility once on stage because you sound like you are buddies with the boss.

- Immediately following your presentation, ask the meeting planner to send a follow-up e-mail from you to the group. You can add a few points that you missed or didn't have time for and direct them to other articles of interest on your website. You can also point them to your online store. If the meeting planner is open to giving you the e-mail addresses, then you may send the e-mail directly to them.
- Use your "Help Me" speech. Sometimes people from other departments or Association Chapters in the audience may see an opportunity. (See Building a Database in Chapter 11.)
- When you are talking to the client about your speech, find out what other meetings take place throughout the year and the purpose of each – you might fit into those as well. Also talk about initiatives that the company is undertaking and plant seeds about what you can help them with. Be careful not to focus too much on future business before you've secured this first booking.
- Thank them for their business after your speech. You might send a gift along with your thank you note at this time or you might wait and send a gift during a holiday. A copy of your book may or may not qualify as a gift. Hopefully by the end of your engagement you know something about them so that you can personalize it. *Note:* Don't cheap out on the gift. If you got paid $5,000 then sending a $25 gift card to Dunkin Donuts isn't going to cut it. Do something classy that stands out. And if you have beautiful Yeti Thermal Coffee mugs with your message on it, even better!
- Schedule your follow-up call to the client a week or ten days after your presentation. There may be some offerings on the "expanding beyond your speech" list that you can offer them right away.
  - Ask them what has changed as a result of your presentation. If they start listing things, ask if you can quote them and send them an e-mail confirming what they said. This prevents you having to wait for a testimonial letter.

- Ask them how you can support them in the future.
- Ask who else they know who could benefit from your material – other departments in their company or other chapters of their association, colleagues, etc. Will they do an introduction?
- Schedule a follow-up call or a note in the future. A quick e-mail asking how things are going six months later may put you in line for more business.

In today's market, we must always be thinking beyond the speech. Yes, the speech may get your foot in the door, but how can you move into a long-term relationship with this client to get the maximum results from your content? Remember the Master's Tip, Selling Beyond the Speech, back in Chapter 12? Go back to that list and ensure that you are exploring all these areas with the client.

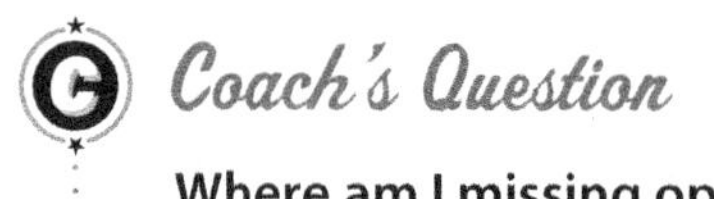

Where am I missing opportunities?

Speaking Agreements and Contracts

Your agreements should be thorough without being a pain in the butt for the meeting organizer. If they have to bring in their legal team to review the agreement, then you may be too intense. You want your agreement to stick, you want your clients to understand all of the money details and what happens if they cancel, but, at the same time, you don't want to scare them off.

In my thirty-plus years, I have yet to hear of a speaker suing a client over a breach of contract. You should do your best to work things out to the client's (and your) satisfaction if they postpone or cancel.

Components of an Agreement

So what needs to go into a contract? Use the checklist below to ensure you include all the pertinent details in your agreement (see Worksheet 18 for a sample agreement. Refer back to these explanations as required.

- Your Name.
- Date of the Agreement.
- Company or Group Name.
- Client's Contact Information – There may be one contact who signs the agreement (primary contact) and another contact on-site at the meeting (on-site contact). Allow the client space to give you both. Be sure to get cell numbers.
- Event Date – You would be surprised how often dates can get mixed up. Putting the date in a specific format – Saturday, November 16, 2024 – can help ensure that there are no mistakes made with the date or day of the week.
- Speech Start Time and Finish Time – Be specific. When you leave these things blank or TBA (to be announced), you leave room for misunderstandings and, when you get busy, this could become a problem.
- Other Time Requirements – If the client would like you to stay for lunch with the audience or participate in an awards ceremony or an autograph session, put it in writing. For celebrity speakers this becomes especially important. Every minute of your time with the client or audience should be put in the agreement.

Putting the date in a specific format – Saturday, November 17, 2024 – can help ensure that there are no mistakes made with the date or day of the week.

- Title of Presentation – Putting this in writing may help you down the road if the client is ever questioning the content of your presentation. Make sure that they know what presentation they are buying.
- Speaking Fee – Place the agreed upon fee here as well as your deposit/payment policy. As you read earlier, most speakers ask for 50% down to hold or reserve the date for the client. The remaining 50% is due on the engagement date. You may send

two invoices – a deposit invoice and a balance invoice due on the engagement date. You will need to schedule a reminder notice for ten days before the event. Your invoices and/or your agreements should include to whom the check is made payable (company or speaker name), address to send check, and Tax I.D. Number. Putting the Tax I.D. up front will save a step later.

- Cancellation Policy – This policy is in place to protect you if the client cancels at the last minute and it also protects the client if you cannot make the engagement. This is your policy, so it's up to you what you ask for, but I'll give you my ideal inclusions. The deposit of 50% is non-refundable unless you (the speaker) cancel. If the client cancels the presentation within forty-five days of the event without rescheduling, then the balance is also non-refundable. You probably won't be able to book another speech to replace this lost income and you may have given up opportunities for paid engagements on this date. Here is some sample language.
  - A non-refundable deposit of $x is due by 00/00/00 to secure and hold the date of your choice. If client cancels forty-five (45) days or less (without immediately rescheduling) before the engagement, the entire fee will be due. Although John Doe Speaker has never missed an engagement, in case of cancellation due to emergency, client will be reimbursed in full.
  - COVID/Force Majeure Clause – This really circles back to your cancellation agreement – what will you do in case of a pandemic or hurricane or other major disruption? I suspect you'll offer them up to a year or eighteen months to reschedule the date. *Note:* My clients' goal during the Pandemic was not only to save the date and the deposit but to book more business to be delivered virtually "in the meantime." They clearly wanted your content, "let's not wait" was the message.
- Venue – Name, address, phone. (You'll want to ask the requirements for shipping books ahead of time; each venue has a shipping policy.)

- Introducer's Name – This may go into the pre-gig questionnaire instead of the agreement. Either way you should gather this information.
- Audio/Video Taping Release – You may allow the client to audio- or videotape your speech, but be sure to ask for a copy for your own use. The video should be used for "internal purposes only and for a limited amount of time" (say ninety days) and not for social media or resale. Putting this in the contract might spur them to arrange for filming when they hadn't thought of it, which is good for you. You should try to film everything. Remember this is your intellectual property so we don't want them to mis-handle it.
- Air Travel – We recommend keeping the booking of the air travel on your "to do" list but consider a *flat rate* for travel to make your and your client's lives easier. With current air travel costs, $1,000 - $1500 might cover it, but you'll have to test that and make sure you aren't losing on each engagement. This flat rate would include air travel, ground transportation, and meals. We do want to keep the booking of the hotel in the clients' hands (see below).
- Hotel Address, Phone (if different from speaking venue) – Typically, the client books the hotel room for the speaker and puts it (and maybe meals) on their room block and master account. The speaker pays for their own incidentals, such as movies, phone calls, etc. Therefore the agreement should spell that out. The agreement should always be clear about who is responsible for making the arrangements.
- Ground Transportation – If you have an all-inclusive travel fee, then you will book the ground transfers in the arriving city. Some clients will want to send a car for you. If that's their preference, then who are we to turn down a limo?
- AV Requirements – An agreement should spell out everything that the client will need to budget for and AV could end up costing a few bucks. Spell out your AV requirements up front on the agreement, rather than have them find out later that you need a projector, comfort monitor, etc. (A comfort monitor is a large screen that goes at the speaker's feet to allow them to see what's

on the audience's big screens as well as their presenter notes.) These items could tack $1000 onto the venue bill so the client needs to know about this at the beginning. You should also ask for the AV company's name either on the agreement or in your pre-gig questionnaire. The idea behind questions like this is - *no surprises.* When you are showing up to speak to 500 people and they intend to use a poor sound system and no professional AV, then you can try to negotiate a better situation for yourself. Sometimes it's the speaker's job to educate the client on how to get the best outcome.

- Handouts/Support Materials - Spell out in the agreement if you are going to provide handouts and if you want the client to arrange for photocopying, etc. If you have agreed to provide 100 books as part of the agreement, this detail should go in as well.

Books for Every Audience

Nowadays there are people who are entirely electronic with their agreements. I love that because it saves trees. And we want to make signing the agreement (e-Sign if possible) as simple as can be. But let's not forget about planting the seed for them to purchase a book for everyone in the audience.

As you are building the relationship, securing the gig, and creating the agreement, this is a great opportunity to suggest deepening the learning with one of your books. It could be that you work this out before going to the agreement phase. But if not, you might overnight a book along with your agreement.

SAMPLE AGREEMENT

Your agreements should be thorough without being a pain in the butt for the meeting planner. You want your agreement to stick, you want your clients to understand all of the money details and what happens if they cancel, but, at the same time, you don't want to scare them off.

Sample Speaker Agreement: Jon Duncan

SPEAKER AGREEMENT

Client Information	
Contact person	Fontana James
Title	VP of Sales
Organization	ITMB Staffing
Address	1444 Garland Rd., Dallas, TX 75226
Phone	214-555-5552 Fax 214-555-5551 Email fontanaj@ITMB.com
Presentation/Workshop Details	
Title	Secrets of the Staffing Wizard
Date	January 21, 20XX
Time	1:00pm – 2:30 pm (90 minute program)
Location	Hotel St. George, Roosevelt Room, 555 Hotel Lane, Dallas, TX 75666
Client Fees and Expenses	
The client agrees to pay the following fees and expenses:	
Fee for this presentation/ workshop	**$7000** A non-refundable 50% deposit of **$3,500** is due by **12/31/XX** to secure the engagement date. If client cancels 45 days or less (without immediately rescheduling) the entire fee will be due as complete settlement. Should the speaker miss the engagement due to illness or emergency and a suitable replacement cannot be found, client will be reimbursed in full. Balance is due on or before the day of engagement.
COVID Clause	We all know that things can change in our world. If there is a reason to postpone this event we will gladly rebook within 2 years. Any deposit or monies paid will be applied to a future event.
Deposit payable to	Duncan Consulting (Tax ID# 04-933333) Address: 555 Wysteria Lane, Austin, TX 76229
Balance payment	The balance of **$3,500** to be handed to the speaker on engagement day.
Travel expenses	Expenses include full coach airfare, meals, ground transportation, and lodging. These expenses will be invoiced after the program. **Jon Duncan** will use his best efforts to keep travel expenses to a minimum.
Support materials	Should the client wish to purchase copies of **Mr. Duncan's** book for each participant, a quantity discount of 40% will apply (sample enclosed). A 6 foot table for back of room is requested for additional support materials and autograph session.
A/V requirements/ audio-video release	Wireless microphone, 6 foot table at back of room. Video recording of Mr. Duncan's presentation is acceptable for internal use only for up to 12 months. In return, we request a high quality master copy of the presentation.

Our signatures on this agreement indicate full compliance with the requests and the promises above, and complete understanding of the services to be provided.

Client: ______________________ Date: ____________

Speaker: ______________________ Date: ____________

wealthyspeakerschool.com

Verbal Agreements

Until you have a signed agreement as well as a deposit check, your agreement is simply a "hold" and should be treated as such. If another client comes sniffing around that date, then call the first client and let them know that their date is not locked in until the paperwork is signed and the deposit is received. If the client is slow in getting the paperwork back to you, it is often a sign of lack of commitment. Do not turn down other engagements or stop taking holds for that date until you have the money in the bank! This is a lesson that I learned the hard way in my early days.

Do not turn down other engagements or stop taking holds for that date until you have the money in the bank!

Bureau Agreements

Speakers' bureaus will often e-mail you a firm offer prior to getting an agreement to you. If the client has signed the firm offer, then it should be as good as a contract. You should receive a formal agreement asking for your signature first and then a fully executed agreement (where all parties – most importantly the client – has signed) later. If you are not sure if the client has signed the contract yet, and have not received a "firm offer" then continue to treat the date as a hold. You will learn early in your work with bureaus that some agents tend to jump the gun and tell you they have a deal before the client has signed the agreement. Believe it when you see it.

All of the same information listed in Worksheet 18 should be on the bureau agreement. Read the fine print on the back of the agreement to make sure you are happy with it and, if not, scratch the paragraph off the agreement and initial it. You should let the bureau agent know ahead of time what you are not comfortable with so they are in the loop at every stage.

Overseas Engagements

When working with organizations overseas, the agreement should be adjusted. You will want to get 100% of your fees and travel in advance. If the money doesn't come through, then you do not get on the plane. You may also request first class flights since you want to arrive at your destination feeling rested. And don't agree to speak the minute you arrive; give yourself a day to recover.

Your fees should double or possibly triple since it's going to take you a day to travel to and from the event city, possibly more. Make sure you are factoring in your time. International work sounds sexy and looks good on your bio, but is often draining. Check it out a few times and then decide how much overseas work is perfect for you in one year.

Also, sadly, you must be aware that there are some overseas scams that have been going around for years. If they don't specifically know why they want you and for what topic, that's a red flag. Ask around. "Did anyone else get this e-mail?" Oftentimes it's an elaborate scam to make you pay for something in order for the deal to go through. Speaker beware!

Ready ✓
Aim ✓
Launch ✓

We've done the heavy lifting, gotten clarity about what we're selling (Ready), developed some marketing materials and the speech (Aim), and rolled out to our target markets (Launch). Fantastic! Next, let's see what we can do to level up our business! Here we go!

GROWING YOUR BUSINESS

Next Level

15

Working with Speakers' Bureaus

That's it for the three ingredients in the Wealthy Speaker Recipe: Ready, Aim, Launch. By this point you should have a clear picture of your expertise and positioning in the marketplace. You should have an awesome speech, your marketing materials should be in place, and your demo video (or clips) should rock. Your database should be growing, and, with great gigs with the perfect clients, working with speakers' bureaus should be on the horizon.

The Big Picture

Many speakers are scratching their heads and wondering how to break into the elusive speakers' bureau network. Either the bureaus never call you or they call and place holds and you never get booked. By the end of this Chapter you should be very clear on when you are ready to work with bureaus, what to expect when you do start, and how to build long-term relationships.

Having worked under the roof of a bureau for six years, I think I can give you a perspective from both the speaker and the bureau.

The bureau business has changed dramatically since I started three decades ago. Google is pretty steep competition. So a bureau needs to capitalize on the trust that they build with their clients. And they don't want to jeopardize that trust by submitting an "unknown" or "unproven" speaker. Not worth it.

It's for this reason that we typically recommend that you build the business on your own first, and look at bureaus once you are Launched. There is the odd exception of course. A speaker with some notoriety (i.e., CEO of a corporation) may go exclusive with a bureau because they actually don't want to build a speaking business. More and more bureaus are opening an "exclusives division" and that might be a match.

The Cost of Doing Business with Bureaus

This is your business and it's your decision who to market to and who to work with. With the odd exception, a speakers' bureau will not launch your business. Most bureaus charge a 25% commission, some will charge 30% on lower fee speakers. The reason many speakers take the bureau partner route is because the more bookings you get, the more your fees can go up. So instead of thinking of it as a loss, think of it as a gain. And, the bureaus may bring you business that you would never have gotten otherwise. You can't market yourself to everyone. A bureau's database is filled with juicy Fortune 100 clients and national associations.

With the odd exception, a speakers' bureau will not Launch your business.

When you start working with bureaus – they might ask if your fee is "gross" or "net." A gross fee is one that is commissionable. A net fee is one that the bureau will add on to and quote a higher price for the client.

The net fee idea is likely not going to come into play for you until you reach $20K or above. Many bestselling authors and celebrities will offer net fees. For instance, a client wants to book a famous daytime talk show host. Let's say she has a net fee of $150K, the bureau might add $25K onto that fee and submit it to the client. The reason this is not done with "normal" speaking fees is that you (the speaker) want to be in charge and have everyone quoting the same fee for you. So my advice is to stick with a gross (commissionable) fee until you are more well known.

You will find that almost every relationship succeeds or fails based on how close your values match up to your partners'. Bureaus are no exception. Work with bureaus who believe in doing business the same way that you do. If you are all about honesty and integrity then find bureaus – or bureau agents – who value those qualities as well.

Find bureaus that have similar values to yours and you will create enjoyable, long-term relationships.

In the early stages of your career, you'll probably take business that you'll regret and you'll work with people that you don't like, but sort through the relationships and reject the ones that aren't working for you. Find bureaus that have similar values to yours and you will create enjoyable, long-term relationships.

A Day in the Life of a Bureau Agent

Understanding that the average bureau agent has a ton of speakers coming at them all day every day can be helpful for someone who wants to get their foot in the door. Recognize that the agent wants to reserve their time for talking to clients booking business (and making money).

Yes, they want to discover new talent, and sometimes have a need for a topic and no speaker to fill it, so they will go "on the hunt." But please know that they might have 10,000 speakers in their database already.

If you really want to get noticed, then get booked directly with their clients. If you are good, bureaus will start to lose business to you and *that* will get their attention.

If you are good, bureaus will start to lose business to you and **that** *will get their attention.*

A speakers' bureau agent may spend months pitching various speakers to a client, only to have the deal mysteriously go away. And the next day a piece of spin-off business falls easily into their lap and books immediately. They work hard, especially during a pandemic where contracts have to be done and redone multiple times for every engagement.

The bottom line? Don't waste their time and be sure you are ready to approach bureaus before reaching out.

Am I Ready for Bureaus – A Checklist

This bears repeating. Unless you're a celebrity in some form, most speakers' bureaus are *not* going to launch your career. They will most likely start paying attention to you after you have built a name for yourself.

To see if you are ready to work with bureaus, ask yourself these four questions.

1. Have I given thirty or more paid speeches per year for at least two years? Or do I have some level of expertise or celebrity that overrides this?
2. Is my fee high enough? When I first got into the business, $10K seemed like a high fee. But today $15,000+ is an average minimum fee for the mid-sized bureaus. Some regional bureaus may have a lower average, so keep that in mind. A bureau like WSB (Washington Speakers Bureau) who represents a lot of celebrities might be booking $25,000 and up. Although at one point they did have a $10K division, I'm not sure if it's still going.
3. Is my demo video ready? And does it sell me?
4. Am I really good? Am I getting two or three spin-off engagements from each speech?

If you wonder why your fee has to be a certain level, it's because bureaus can't make bank on a $300 commission. Anything under $10K for them – that's a $2500 commission that is split between the owner and the agent – might not feel worthwhile based on their overhead.

Where Do I Find the Bureaus?

If you feel that your topic and approach is unique enough to get noticed by bureaus, the easiest way to start is with the International Association of Speakers' Bureaus (IASB). They have a website and you can use their "Find a Member" search feature. From there, you'll want to do some research

to narrow the list to bureaus who meet your criteria. Some criteria might include: they work with speakers in my genre and fee range; they have a great reputation in the industry, both with speakers and clients; and they have the type of clients that I want to work with. There is no point getting listed with a bureau that does all college work when you have no desire to speak to colleges.

Getting Your Foot in the Door

The best scenario is for the bureau to have heard your name three times (preferably from clients or from other speakers) prior to you calling them. Have your clients and speaker buddies do an introduction. Clients hold much more water when it comes to referrals.

Once a speakers' bureau loses business to you on multiple occasions, they will take notice.

"I got listed with ABC speakers' bureau!"

That's a good start. But know that "getting listed," getting on their website, means very little really. You are placed in their database with the other thousands of speakers. This is just the very first step in building your bureau relationship. Most bureaus post their requirements for getting listed with them on their websites. Check out the website first, then call and make sure your topic and fees are in line with what they book. If they give you the thumbs up, then e-mail over your information.

Note: If you are listed on eSpeakers, the bureau can often pull your information right into their database. There is also an option to do a Bureau Blast on eSpeakers (a paid service) that has been a good investment for some of my clients.

Theresa Beenken, of National Speakers Bureau in Toronto, says clients and bureaus are looking to book *you* because of *your* style, *your* experience, *your* content and how it will benefit their audience.

Staying Top of Mind

As discussed above, getting listed is the first step. Now you want to take the relationship further. You need to stay in touch, but not become a stalker or pest. Every bureau will have their own preferences on how to be contacted, so make notes in your database and try to accommodate their wishes.

- **Phone** – Calling to touch base during an agent's sales hours is probably not ideal, unless you have something important to say. Leaving after hours voice messages could be effective, however.
- **E-mail** – The average number of e-mails a bureau agent receives per day is staggering. So when sending e-mail, make sure it has value for them, keep it short with links to more information, and never send anything weekly (e.g., a newsletter) unless asked. Do not add a bureau to your newsletter list without their permission.
- **Mail** – Sending your book, postcards, and notes via old-fashioned snail mail also works.
- **In Person** – Don't drop in unexpectedly. See if they want to host an "agent lunch" with you and you can tell them about yourself while providing pizza or sandwiches or sushi for everyone.
- **Invite them to a gig** – If you are speaking in their home city, see if someone from the office will come out and view your presentation. That's a great way to get your foot in the door, especially if you can introduce them to a new client.

Do not add a bureau to your newsletter list without their permission.

You'll need to work hard to keep the bureau's attention. The more creative you can be the better. Below are some ideas to get the bureau agent's attention.

SHOWCASES

If the bureau has showcases (which typically cost you money), that is a good way to gain some exposure to the bureau. Ideally, you want that bureau's agents, as well as their clients, to see you in action. Ask several speakers how many engagements they booked as a result of previous showcases before you pay your money.

If you are an unknown speaker and a bureau approaches you to showcase with them, be *very* cautious. They may be making more money from the showcases than from actually booking speakers.

IASB has their own showcase during their annual convention. If you are working with some bureaus who are members, they might be able to get you into the showcase – in front of all of the bureau agents and owners. There is another option to become a sponsor for the event. But the best-case scenario is to have a bureau champion you as a main stage speaker at that event.

*If you are an unknown speaker and a bureau approaches you to showcase with them, be **very** cautious.*

This past year one of my private coaching clients, Gaby Natale, a Latina bestselling author and speaking pioneer, submitted a proposal to speak at IASB. They liked her so much they placed her as the closing speaker at the Annual Convention. A huge game changer in her business.

HANDING OVER BUSINESS

Another way to get noticed by a bureau is to hand them a deal that you have already closed. This might work if you are already close to getting in with the bureau and just want to tip it over the edge. But if the bureau doesn't know you from Adam, and hasn't expressed any interest in you to date, I'd hold off giving away that 25%.

SPIFFS AND CONTESTS

A "spiff" is a contest or promotion that you would offer to the bureau agents to get them to book you more often. It might come in the form of a gift, like an Amazon gift card, a trip, etc. I've even seen some speakers offer cash. The idea is that the bureau agent who books the speaker the most would win. Sometimes there could be more than one winner.

If you are going to try something like this (and please note it may not fly), then make sure you get the owner of the bureau's blessing first. Because most bureau agents will put their clients' needs well above any incentive you can dangle in front of them, this may be seen as unethical or unseemly.

Closing the Business

If a bureau has placed you on hold multiple times without a booking, there could be two issues at hand: 1) they don't know exactly how to position and sell you or 2) your marketing (website and video) is not competing to win.

If it's your marketing, then you will hear this from more than one bureau and know that your video (and possibly your speech) needs some work. If it's the former, then you might ask if you can spend fifteen minutes on a Zoom meeting with the bureau agents to help improve the closing ratio.

It's a very common issue for bureaus not to "get" what a speaker does. After all, they may have thousands upon thousands of speakers in their database. How can they possibly know every one? Make sure your marketing materials are doing their job and schedule a chat if needed.

The best way for a bureau rep to understand your work is to see you live. And if they are really sharp, they are asking you what you can offer outside of speeches and will get a commission on the added value stuff. Not sure how many bureau agents think creatively (beyond booking one *speech*), but when you get someone who does, build the relationship ... cause they're a keeper!

Being a Partner

Once you have booked an engagement, keep the agent in the loop while working with the client at every stage of the preparation. After the event, introduce the bureau agent to the decision-makers you've met on-site and allow that relationship to unfold. The bureau may get opportunities for business they would not have received without your introduction.

Trust Your Partner

Issues that involve trust will arise over the course of working with bureaus. It's bound to happen. A bureau should trust that you are, indeed, going to hand over any spin-off business, just as you have to trust that they will follow up the leads that you give them.

The best long-term relationships are relaxed and involve mutual trust. A good motto for both bureaus and speakers is "do the right thing, even if no one is looking." If you are not confident that a bureau is representing you properly, then have a discussion with them to clarify roles. Over time, the bureaus that you enjoy working with will be the ones who book you most.

Spin-off

A good motto for both bureaus and speakers is "do the right thing, even if no one is looking."

All business that results from a bureau engagement goes back to the bureau. Notice I said *all business* – not some or occasionally. Without this initial piece of business, you would not have the spin-off. This may also apply to bulk product sales. Some bureaus will ask for 10% or 20% commission on books.

How you handle "the spin" may depend on your relationship. You might have an agreement with the bureau agent that you'll close the business and hand it back to them for the contract. Or they may want you to send spin-off right away to see if there is more business to be nurtured. Either way, the booking should go back to them.

A few years back if you'd asked twenty bureau agents who their favorite speaker was, many of them would have said Joe Calloway. Why? Not only did he track his spin-off voraciously, he'd make sure a bureau received a spin-off even if twenty years had passed. On top of that, Joe's ability to be memorable on the platform had clients asking for him a decade later! Read more about Joe in Chapter 16.

The reason this is in past tense is that Joe has come off the road and is spending his time consulting and working with start-ups and other projects that interest him. His speaking business built his ability to do whatever he wants with his free time these days! Sweet!

Heading Off Problems at the Pass

If you have any issues with clients about travel or AV expenses, try to address them up front. For instance, air travel that costs over $1,000 may be a big issue for clients. If you don't bill an all-inclusive travel fee (recommended) let the bureau agent know what your travel is going to cost (roughly) at the time of the booking so that they can educate the client. The last thing you want is for your final contact with the client to be one that is negative.

Any problems with an engagement should be faced head on with a Zoom chat, phone call, or e-mail to the bureau agent. "I don't agree to the client's recording clause" or "There's an extra cost for the comfort monitor" or "My flight is delayed" or "The books didn't arrive."

Leaving the client or bureau in the dark about anything is not a good policy.

All of these items should be discussed as they happen. Leaving the client or bureau in the dark about anything is not a good policy.

Getting Paid

Most bureaus will mail your speaking fee to you within two weeks after the engagement. If you are not being paid reasonably quickly by bureaus, call them to find out why. Be the squeaky wheel. Although many do not send a portion of the deposit they receive, they should have received full payment from the client before the event date. If not, then they are not staying on top of things. If you feel uncomfortable working with a bureau because of delayed payment, then don't. It's like any business - you choose who to work with and who not to work with.

For more specifics on deposits, agreements or cancellations, see Chapter 14 at Agreements and Contracts.

Recently one of my students told me about a booking with a bureau where he hadn't been paid, and he knew that the bureau had received payment from the client. The bureau was in financial trouble and my client was about to sue them. I told him that before taking it to court, he should make an effort to have a candid conversation with the bureau owner about his intentions to sue, which he did.

During the conversation, the bureau owner confessed that they had been having a rough quarter and they set up a payment schedule that was satisfactory to my client. Relationships mean a lot in the speaking industry. And knowing that bureau the way I did, I knew they were not being deceitful on purpose. People get into trouble. The lesson here is always proceed with caution before getting in too deep with an agency that is holding on to your money for you. And ask other speakers if they have been paid in a timely manner. Any bureau that is notorious for slow payments should be handled with caution (and believe me I know a little about this as the bureau I once worked for went bankrupt). But please know that for every one bureau with cash flow problems, there are nine who are doing just fine and always pay on time.

Bottom Line on Bureaus

Don't expect that the bureaus will be the answer to your prayers. With the odd exception, they rarely Launch or build anyone's speaking business to a major degree in the early days. Go out and book the business yourself first, and the bureaus will take notice. I know, I said this before, but it is important to absorb.

Bureaus are a great way to build your name recognition in the industry and create demand so that your fee goes up. Once you get to the top, don't forget who helped you get there. Keep the lines of communication open, stay in touch, and operate in the spirit of partnership and you will have brilliant bureau relationships that last a long time!

Who Else Might You Partner With?

There are many different types of agencies that help in the planning of an event. As you get more and more into the speaking business, you'll, no doubt, run across them. If you can establish a relationship, some of these may turn fruitful.

- **Partner with Your Local VCB.** The Visitors and Convention Bureaus have a list of the conferences that are coming to town. You might become a member (usually cheap) and get to know the players in the meetings industry in your backyard.
- **Production Companies.** Every time you do a speech that includes a table of people at the back of the room wearing headsets and controlling the AV, you want to ingratiate yourself to this team. They might recommend you for future engagements, especially if you are professional and easy to work with. (Don't be a diva.) They could also be your hook up to getting a copy of the video quickly. Some speakers carry around $50 Amazon gift cards for this exact purpose. *Note:* Some production companies, like Heroic Productions in Minneapolis, even have their own speakers' bureau.

- **Destination Management Companies.** The first thing that a large corporate or association event needs is a destination and some organizations will farm out the task of finding the venue(s). You might check in with some DMs to see if they ever need a line on local speakers.

- **Event Management Companies.** There are businesses out there serving the event market who provide everything from registration to name badges to signage to promotions of an event. And everything in between. Perhaps you partner and become their "go-to" speaker when the topic is right!

- **Association Management Companies.** There are organizations that manage multiple, sometimes dozens, of associations. And associations run events, so perhaps you partner with them and become a great resource for multiple conferences.

- **In-House Speakers' Bureaus.** There are some pretty major players who have their own speakers' bureaus. Perhaps you write an article for *Fortune* magazine and become a part of their in-house speakers' bureau. Many of the big publishing houses have bureaus. Some large associations offer their members access to a list of speakers.

Bottom line: When you partner with people, have the end goal in mind. What are they trying to accomplish with this event? And be aware that you are just a small, small cog in the wheel of that meeting. Kris Campbell of Heroic Productions says, "I notice more and more that speakers who make working with them *easy* are the ones with whom meeting planners want to work. If the speaker considers the customers' desired outcome, then we've hit the jackpot!"

KAREN HARRIS (CMI SPEAKERS)

The Advantage of Partners

For over twenty years, we've had the honor and privilege of working with speakers' bureaus from around the world. When I first started in the industry, I was working with Alan Hobson and Jamie Clarke, two extraordinary Everest climbers who used their speaking careers to change thousands of lives. When I learned about speakers' bureaus from Alan, Jamie, and Jane Atkinson, it made total sense to find more people that could spread the word about their message.

As there was only one of me and since I was new to the industry, I sought out relationships with speakers' bureaus right from the start. I found my tribe – a group of people who were willing to help a newbie like me. Those relationships have brought me much value and life-long friendships with people who truly care about changing the world, one speech at a time.

Over the years, these relationships have helped me to launch and enhance all of our speakers' business growth. We've been blessed to have a number of our speakers grace the main stage at their annual IASB conference, to have various bureaus welcome our speakers at their office, and to have agents trust us with allowing prospects to preview our speakers at their events.

Today, the bureau industry is more complex. Some bureaus have only exclusive speakers; some have no exclusive speakers; some have "managed" speakers (meaning other bureaus can book them without co-brokering on commissions); and there are all kinds of combinations of these categories.

Regardless of what type of bureau you might be interested in working with, they won't build your business for you. To get noticed by speakers' bureaus, you need a few very key ingredients: a large digital footprint; positioning that clearly defines the problem(s) you solve; and a reputation for integrity in your business dealings.

16

Growing Your Business

The discussion that follows in this Chapter will allow you to continue to grow your business further to continue to work towards The Perfect Day in Your Life (remember Worksheet 3). Check out my book, *Scaling Your Business*, for a deeper dive on some of these areas.

Here are a few ideas on how to expand your revenue.

- Write a Book
- Develop on Online Course
- Create an App
- Deliver Consulting/Advisory Work
- Start a Membership Community
- Start a Mastermind
- Deliver Coaching
- Follow-Up Video Series
- Live Events
- Retreats

All the items on this list could be a book or course unto itself. I recommend that if you, for instance, want to learn how to build an online course, you find the best people and learn from them. Amy Porterfield is my "go-to" for online revenue streams. Check out her podcast "Online Marketing Made Easy." She also introduced me to Stu McLaren who is the guru of memberships.

Some of the lower hanging fruit on this list are coaching and consulting. You already have some processes and formulas in place because of your presentations, could you go deeper on those? Don't be afraid to do Beta testing with clients to see what works and what doesn't. A year-long coaching program is what delivers the best results for my clients, but you (like some of my students) might find a year waaaaaay too long. Test things in shorter time frames and see what you love and gets results for your clients.

Don't be afraid to do Beta testing with clients to see what works and what doesn't.

Because books are such a huge part of a speaker's journey, we'll dive deep into this section. If you're not at all interested in writing a book, then skip forward.

Write a Book

Writing a book does several things for you and is indeed a "flashpoint" moment. It establishes your expertise and credibility. It allows you to document your ideas, your formula or recipe for success, and, of course, can be an income stream.

Choosing How to Publish

There are some difficult decisions to be made about how to publish your book. Many people these days are opting for the self-publishing route for a few reasons (see the Publishing Quiz, Worksheet 19). They want to get the book to print quickly, make more money, and have more control.

But if you have the desire to have a "bestselling" book or you feel you want the credibility behind you of a big-nwame publishing house, you might want to consider the traditional or hybrid routes.

PUBLISHING QUIZ

Before you decide how to publish your book, get clear on the type of book you want. A "Back of Room Make Money" book is a product that you sell at speeches when your audience simply wants to take a piece of you home with them. Or even better when the decision-maker pre-purchases a book for everyone in the audience. An Expert/Bestseller book helps to establish serious credibility in the marketplace and appeals to a broader range of readers. Take the quiz to see which route is perfect for you.

Keep three considerations in mind when deciding which way to publish your book: time, credibility, and profit. Complete the quizzes to determine which method will work for you.

Option One – Expert Bestseller Book (Traditional Publisher)

1. I want to be nationally recognized as a leading expert in my field.
2. I want to sell my books all over the world.
3. I want to have a shot at writing a bestseller.
4. I do not care how long it takes to publish my book.
5. I do not care how much money I make on my book (traditionally $1/book).
6. I'm okay giving up some creative control and licensing "rights" on my book.
7. I want my book to be in a wide range of bookstores.

Option Two – Back of Room Make Money Book (Self-Publish)

1. I want my clients and prospects to see me as credible.
2. I want to have something to sell before or at my speeches.
3. I don't care if my book gets into bookstores (or I'll secure distribution myself).
4. I want to make good money from my book? ($7-10/book).
5. I want my book to be published quickly.
6. I want 100% creative control over the process and own all the "rights."
7. I'll sell my book myself on my website, back of room, and Amazon.

Option 3 – Hybrid Book

1. I want to have creative control and keep the "rights" to my book.
2. I want to make decent money on my books ($5-$7/book).
3. I want my book published reasonably quickly.
4. I want my book to get into bookstores.
5. I can afford to put some serious investment behind my book ($10-$40K).
6. I want my clients and prospects to see me as credible.
7. I'll also sell my book myself on my website, back of room, and Amazon.

The hybrid option is one of the most expensive of all of the options. But it gives you more distribution than the self-publishing model. And you may have a quality name publisher (e.g., Greenleaf Publishing) on the cover which adds credibility. (I have published with Greenleaf before and they are quite reputable.)

There is more prestige in going with a big-name publisher, but the odds of a publisher picking up your book are somewhat skewed. Some people say you need an agent to secure a deal like this, but I've seen them done directly as well. A bestselling book could be the difference between a $5,000 keynote fee and a $25,000 fee, but again, the odds of making the bestseller list are not stacked in your favor considering that more than 500,000 books are published each year. Clients may see a big-name publisher as more credible than self-publishing, although I think that has really changed over the years as self-publishing grows.

You have to weigh all of the pros and cons and look at your goals. If you go the publisher route, remember that finding a literary agent and writing a book proposal can take eight to twelve months alone. You don't always need a lit agent to get a publisher. But remember, you still have to write the book!

Personally, I am big on self-publishing because it allows me to get paid what I'm worth and the timeline is my own. The original version of *The Wealthy Speaker* went from idea to book in hand in under twelve months. That would never have happened with a publishing house. I've had publishers approach me about doing a "Speaking for Dummies" type book, but just couldn't bring myself to sign off on an agreement that was so one sided. The author has no control, the publisher has it all.

If you choose self-publishing, be sure to run low print numbers to begin with until you see how your book is selling. The last thing you want is a thousand books in your basement gathering cobwebs years from now. Print-on-demand allows you to keep your initial orders low and saves on money and storage. And pre-selling your book (advanced copies) can allow you to judge how many should be in that initial order.

Print-on-demand allows you to keep your initial orders low and saves on money and storage.

The Co-Authoring Option

I just received an e-mail asking if I would like to co-author a book with twenty-eight other authors. First, the organizer didn't do their homework. If they knew I had already written six of my own books, they'd know that I'm not at all interested in this idea. Why would I want to promote twenty-eight other people as experts?

The second problem I have with these projects is that no one person is really in charge of selling these books. The organizers require each author to purchase a minimum number of books, so I'm going to guess that the organizer makes money but many of those books don't get sold. Because as soon as you write your own book, that will be your number one priority.

There's the odd time when this option might work for you. If you don't ever want to write your own book, it's aligned with some thought leaders that you admire, or you want to put "author" after your name sooner than later. Cool, go for it!

And if you've participated in a book like this already, perhaps you made it work quite nicely for yourself.

Selling Product

When selling product from the platform, find the method that best suits your style, your audience, and, most importantly, your client. When you lead with value, everyone wins. Even better. Pre-sell the books so that every member of the audience gets to take a piece of you home!

Back of Room

There are ways to sell "back of room" that will leave the audience and client happy. If the client really wants your message to go deep, then perhaps they purchase a book for everyone and you can hold an "autograph session" afterwards. Notice I say "autograph session" instead of "book signing" as it sounds more celebrity-like.

But if they don't want to pre-purchase, perhaps you ask for a six-foot table at the back of the room and request a volunteer from the audience to help you run your sales. When you can stand at one end of the table signing books, and someone else is running the credit cards, that is brilliant. Card readers like Square make it very easy to collect money. But keep your numbers round (e.g., $20/book) to allow for easy cash transactions and don't forget to take any sales tax into consideration.

You can direct people to where you will be after your presentation during your speech, and reference your book subtly (i.e., "There's a story I tell in the book where ..." or "On page 59 in the book I reference ..."). You can also have the meeting organizer or MC pitch your book for you. What you don't want is a twenty-minute sales pitch.

There is a speaker in the industry who is a huge bestselling author and very famous. When a meeting planner said to me, "We had a bad experience with a speaker selling product from the stage last year," I knew immediately who they were talking about. Regardless of the value that this speaker was creating for his audiences, all the client remembered was that he flogged his products from the platform for 25% of the time that he was paid – extremely well – to speak. Think about it this way. If this speaker was paid $25,000 for a sixty-minute keynote, he was receiving $415 per minute. He spent 15 minutes – or $6250 – serving himself, rather than his audience. Not good!

Website Sales

Of course, back of the room is just one way to sell your product. Selling on your website is another option. The key requirements are a shopping cart and a credit card gateway. Try to find an option that is as simple to use and hassle free as possible. We've used a bunch of different set ups over the years, but have landed with ThriveCart (great for coaches) and Stripe (which offers both US and Canadian currencies). Those both work well on my WordPress site. You can start with PayPal and move to a less expensive option over time.

Whichever options you take, remember that selling books in bulk is the best way to make money from your products. Work them into your packages. Raising up your keynote fee by adding books is a far better use of your time than selling one book at a time on your website.

Sidenote: For the first twenty years of my business, we kept all the shipping of books in-house. I had a fulfillment house in Michigan that shipped out the orders as they came in. This allowed me to collect the names and e-mail addresses of my readers. But recently we got out of the shipping business and have started handing things over to Amazon. Let them do the shipping as they were difficult to compete with anyway. I don't get the names and e-mail addresses, but when people sign up for the download we overcome that obstacle.

JOE CALLOWAY

Growing Your Wealth Beyond Gigs

The thirty-plus years that I spent as a keynote speaker were good to me. Very, very good to me. My business was successful, I worked with wonderful people (bureaus, clients, colleagues), and I made lifelong friends.

There is also life beyond speaking! I am now an advisor to executives, solo professionals, and entrepreneurs. I'm also a partner in two real estate groups that build and sell condo and apartment developments. Gilson Snow is a winter sports product company in which I was an original investor and where I still remain active as an owner and advisor to the executive team. My newest venture is as a partner in the Barrel Stock Trading Company. We buy, age, and sell Kentucky Straight Bourbon to distillers and blenders.

I would advise any speaker to invest as much of your speaking income as possible in projects that will create income for you forever. One of the most successful (and wealthy) speakers that I ever knew once told me that you don't get truly wealthy from speaking fees. You get truly wealthy by investing those speaking fees.

You don't get truly wealthy from speaking fees. You get truly wealthy by investing those speaking fees.

Hiring a Team

With a few exceptions, most of the Wealthy Speakers in the field (top 10%) have a great marketing person or team behind them. When Vince and I were still working together, people always asked him, "How do I find 'a Jane?'" Back in the day, Tony Alessandra had Holli Catchpole (my idol when I first started in the industry) who went on to manage multiple speakers via her company, SpeakersOffice. Ryan Estis teamed up with Lynn Mandinec and the list goes on.

Today, hiring a VA (Virtual Assistant) is pretty commonplace. Grooming one to work with you for years to help you grow your business is next level. Perhaps we start small and build from there.

The hiring process has six considerations.

1. Are you ready to hire?
2. What should this person do for you?
3. How much should you pay?
4. Who is the right fit?
5. Where will you find them?
6. Will they be "in house" or virtual.

Solve Your Problems First, then Hire

One of the most common things I hear from professional speakers is that they are not interested in selling themselves. They'd like to hire someone to do it for them. And I'll tell you that it's a difficult thing to do successfully. Why? Because if a speaker doesn't know how to sell themselves how are they going to train someone else to do it for them?

So, first you need to fix the problem, then you hire someone to implement the solution.

If you put your Launch systems in place and test them and get some bookings yourself, then you can hire someone to do the same. Placing the burden of fixing your business on someone else's shoulders is a big cross to bear.

Placing the burden of fixing your business on someone else's shoulders is a big cross to bear.

Start Slow and Build

A terrific idea I heard on a podcast is to give a prospective employee a project or assignment to start. Let's say you have three people who are on your short list for hiring. Assign them all the same task and see who comes back with the best results. I love starting slow with a VA and building from there.

My amazing assistant Monica (who's pretty much my right arm) started with managing my live events first (securing hotel, name tags, registration, menu). Then, we added the podcast onto her list (securing guests, promoting, working with the production house). Then she took over customer service for my school students (onboarding new students, fielding questions) and then we added the school's group coaching calendar (managing class scheduling, guest experts, posting events in our community). It was a slow build and she documented SOPs (standard operating procedures) as we went.

Monica is local to me, which means that we can meet once a month (or however often we like) to run through things. I can't tell you how much it means to sit across from someone and talk about your plans in person. Decide ahead of time whether or not you want that in your assistant. You might even have them come into your office if that's your preference.

When you hire, think of it in three categories, with three price points. Please note these may have increased depending on when you are reading this book.

- Sales $$$ – they are making you money
- Business Assistant $$ – they are focused on business administration

- Personal Assistant $ – they help keep your life on track

Your salesperson has the ability to bring you the most value. You could offer them a small base and a percentage of your bookings (say 10%). Be careful not to start feeding them tasks from the business or personal assistant's lists. You want your salesperson focused on revenue-generating activities and having them making changes to your website or newsletter is going to be a distraction.

With your business assistant, the pay scale goes up with technical skills. Think $25/hour up to $75/hour. Having someone clean up and then manage your CRM is well worth the price but probably at the lower end of the scale since it's not difficult work.

Your personal assistant is more like minimum wage to $25/hour. If they really enhance your life, perhaps $30. Imagine someone picking up your dry cleaning, bringing fresh flowers once a week, or running your kids to class.

A note on overseas hiring. I really love working with people close to my own time zone. But I also love the opportunity to be generous with an overseas assistant. Someone whose life and family are made remarkably better because you paid them a $50 bonus at the end of the project or on a holiday. For someone in the Philippines, $50 might mean putting food on the table for their family, and we all need to remember that.

DEVELOPING A JOB DESCRIPTION

BONUS DOWNLOAD

One of the biggest mistakes speakers make when hiring is not getting clear on their needs until after they have hired. You need to be clear on what tasks you want this person to perform for you. Do you want someone to run your administration? Or someone to do outbound marketing? Do you want someone to pick up your dry cleaning? Or are you looking for a combination? Use the list of tasks to determine what your assistant should do. The lists are broken down into categories: getting speaking engagements, administrative duties, and personal assistant. At the end of the worksheet you will have the basis for a job description.

Getting Speaking Engagements

- [ ] Prospecting
- [ ] Cold calling
- [ ] Marketing to and working with bureaus
- [ ] Developing or updating marketing materials
- [ ] Sending out e-mails
- [ ] Proposals (writing, designing, sending out)
- [ ] Closing deals (overcoming objections, etc.)
- [ ] Meeting with clients
- [ ] Showcase events
- [ ] Following up leads from gigs
- [ ] New product development

Administrative Duties

- [ ] Booking travel
- [ ] Generating invoices/bookkeeping
- [ ] Schedule management
- [ ] Gig logistics
- [ ] Product fulfillment (shipping)
- [ ] Database management
- [ ] Newsletter management
- [ ] Website management
- [ ] Managing other business interests/investments, etc.

Personal Assistant

- [ ] Picking up dry cleaning
- [ ] Feeding the fish
- [ ] Keeping you organized
- [ ] Arranging for babysitters
- [ ] Shopping
- [ ] Arranging family trips, etc.

Where Do I Find Them?

Now that you have a vision of your assistant in mind, here are some places to look for them.

- **Your Inner Circle** – Put out a notice (on social media or word of mouth) for the type of person you are seeking to everyone you know in your business and personal life. Perhaps someone in your networking group or church knows someone who needs a job.
- **Your Audience** – Often someone who comes to talk to you after a presentation might be a candidate. You might even mention it from the platform.
- **VA Association** – Search your local virtual assistant association. Nationally they can be found at IVAA.org.

Bottom Line on Hiring

Keep in mind the principle "hire slow, fire fast." Take your time. Be prepared to spend a lot of time training this person. This is why it's so important for you to know how to book speaking business. Do not bring them in, leave them alone, and expect them to start booking business for you. That, most likely, won't happen. Have them come out to several of your speeches, read your books, watch your videos. Let them listen to you and role play with you prior to picking up the phone. Have a training agenda.

Do not bring them in, leave them alone, and expect them to start booking business for you.

Hiring is like a marriage and the stats might even be similar (50%+ failure rate). Be a great leader to your team. When hiring, take your time, visualize the perfect person coming into your business, and give them the training and tools to be successful.

The High-Tech Speaker on the Road

I can't stress enough to beginning speakers that keeping your business simple in the early days is imperative. You can add bells and whistles with technology as you go. The majority of your income in the first few years should be spent on the speech and marketing.

Here are a few tools of the trade for the ultimate high-tech speaker.

- Smart Phone
- Laptop. Don't forget your chargers and dongles/adapters, especially for Mac users.
- Presentation Software. You can use PowerPoint, Keynote, Prezi, or something similar.
- Wireless Remote for advancing slides
- Business card scanning App
- Trip-it or eSpeakers Apps – keep all of your travel/speech details in one location
- Credit card swipe App for back of room sales

Making Time for Your Body While on the Road

A speaker named Jason Womack told me years ago that when he travels, instead of setting up his computer on the desk in the hotel room, he lays out his workout clothes. That way, rather than getting sucked into the computer (which we think will only be fifteen minutes, but usually turns into two hours), he goes to the gym or for a run instead. These are the types of tips that road warriors need to know in order to thrive out there.

Plan out your travel days just as if you were at home and make sure that you plan some healthy activities. Some speakers speed walk at airports, some take their own food on the road, while others do yoga in their room, or use the hotel swimming pool. Don't leave your health to chance while on the road or, before you know it, you'll be feeling the negative effects of being a road warrior.

Go Get 'Em

Who motivates the motivators? When you have stood in front of hundreds or thousands of people over the course of the year, it's easy to start to buy into the hype. "Hey, I'm a pretty big deal." But what if you are struggling? What if you are having some doubts about yourself?

Well, I'm here to tell you that keeping it real is the way to go. You don't have to be the superhero wearing the cape 24/7. Have some people in your corner who you can be honest with and who will give it right back to you. Join us over at The Wealthy Speaker School. We have students there who are thriving but we also have some who are struggling. And oftentimes, our coaches are able to identify when there is a "mindset disconnect" or a strategic pivot that is required.

My own journey has been one of ups and downs. Times of high confidence and abundance interspersed with short periods of operating from scarcity and fear; that's to be expected over three decades in the speaking business. Twenty years with my own company, we've seen some sh%t go down! I can't even begin to tell you how many things we've tried and failed. And I don't want to tell you how many times I wanted to pack it all in. But giving up is just not who I am, and I suspect it's not who you are either.

When I landed in the industry, I was intimidated to be around so many superstars. But slowly, over time I began to step out from behind my speakers, and into the spotlight myself. Are there times when I feel "less than?" Oh yes! I get coached on it frequently. But knowing that I can fall back on the people who have my back, and that I can be honest about *not feeling quite so superhero-like today* keeps the anxiety at bay.

So keep it real people. You can take off your cape once in a while.

You can take off your cape once in a while.

When I think about writing the first version of this book well over a decade ago, I think about what's changed in my life. I went from being single with no kids to being married with two step-daughters and now six grandkids, three boys, three girls. I'm called G-Ma. I went from having a small condo, walking by the gorgeous houses along the river and dreaming big dreams to owning one of those big houses. And to purchasing a cottage on a lake where we'll watch our grandkids grow up waterskiing and wakeboarding. How cool is that?

I went from earning $35,000 in my first year as a coach to multiplying that income by more than ten times and I'm still growing. The Wealthy Speaker School started with five students, we now have seventy-five and are on the path to many more. And yes, we've tried lots of things that didn't work, until they did. My fees for coaching have gone from $1500 to $15,000 and my programs have just gotten more and more robust.

My team and I have literally helped thousands of speakers build the businesses of their dreams, many earning their first $100,000, $350,000, and $500,000 – and several even moving into multi-seven figure businesses.

Failure is pretty much the only path to success. You get out there and start marketing yourself as a speaker, and what do you get? Crickets. So what do you do? You change it up and go back again. You give some free speeches. Maybe you deliver some freebies to audiences that are the wrong fit, that's okay. All stage time is good stage time. Perhaps you have some flops – we've all done it. You keep going. You keep speaking. Remember, there are only two things required for success – mindset and consistent action.

You know I like to bottom line things. And the bottom line on this, Wealthy Speakers, is you've got to get Ready, take Aim, and Launch. And if it doesn't work, you Launch again. And you keep going until it does work. Until you become The Wealthy Speaker!

I hope you'll reach out and connect because I want to hear about your Wealthy Speaker Journey!

Gratitude for My Peeps

I cannot tell you how much I appreciate all of my peers and colleagues in the speaking industry. To name them all would take too long, but I do want to say that pretty much everything I know about speaking came from conversations in the hallway (or at the bar) at an industry convention. Thank you to CAPS (Canadian Association of Professional Speakers) and NSA (National Speakers Association) for providing those forums for learning.

My book team Catherine Leek of Green Onion Publishing and my designer Kim Monteforte, you are simply gems and I've loved working with you both over two decades and seven projects.

My day-to-day team – Monica Martin, my right *and* left arms, and Jen McDonough who runs our school – I would be lost without you. Sarah Nascimento, Marc Haine, and my crew at Pibworth Professional Services – thank you so much for giving us your time and talent!

To all of the contributors to this book, thank you for your generosity.

And most importantly to my husband John, my greatest love and biggest fan, I'm so happy you are on my team! And I can't wait for our next chapter! To our kids and grandkids, I love you and aspire to be a role model of someone living life on their own terms!

And to the speaker who reaches out tomorrow and says, "I'm going to be your next superstar!!" To you I say, "Yeah, you will!!! Go get 'em!" I hope I see you in one of our programs soon!

Other Books by

JANE ATKINSON

TO ORDER:
www.speakerlauncher.com

THE WEALTHY SPEAKER DAILY SUCCESS PLANNER AND JOURNAL

THE EPIC KEYNOTE

Presentation Skills and Styles of Wealthy Speakers

SCALING YOUR SPEAKING BUSINESS

10 Strategies for Earning More While Doing Less

And Now

THE WEALTHY SPEAKER 3.0

Made in the USA
Monee, IL
16 August 2023

41141543R00142